LEARNING THE SKILLS OF PEACEMAKING

REVISED AND EXPANDED

A K-6 ACTIVITY GUIDE ON
RESOLVING CONFLICT,
COMMUNICATING,
COOPERATING

by Naomi Drew

Foreword by Yogesh K. Gandhi

LEARNING THE SKILLS OF PEACEMAKING

REVISED AND EXPANDED

A K-6 ACTIVITY GUIDE ON
RESOLVING CONFLICT,
COMMUNICATING,
COOPERATING

by Naomi Drew

Foreword by Yogesh K. Gandhi

JP

JALMAR PRESS
Carson, California

Learning the Skills of Peacemaking, Revised And Expanded

Copyright © 1995 by Naomi Drew

Published by Jalmar Press

LEARNING THE SKILLS OF PEACEMAKING, REVISED AND EXPANDED

Author: Naomi Drew
Editor: Susan Remkus
Project Director: Jeanne Iler
Illustrator: Jacqueline Lamer Lockwood
Designer: Susan Brewer
Production of Revision: Electronic Publishing Services, Inc. and Julia Tempel Olsen
Manufactured in the United States of America
Library of Congress Number: 87-81609
First edition printing 1987, eight printings.
Revised printing 1995: 10 9 8 7 6 5 4 3
The new *Learning the Skills of Peacemaking* is a totally revised and updated edition.
ISBN: 1-880396-42-4

WHAT OTHERS HAVE TO SAY...

"Learning the Skills of Peacemaking is an excellent resource for conflict resolution and peacemaking. Naomi Drew has adapted the techniques of negotiation to the needs of children. If everyone learned these peacemaking guidelines in their childhood, the world would be a better place. People of all ages will benefit from this book."

MICHIKO KURODA
The United Nations

"I am deeply touched that my book *Human Options* figured in your decision to create *Learning the Skills of Peacemaking*, and I offer you every good wish with this important undertaking."

NORMAN COUSINS

"I want to express my sincere admiration and support for your excellent program. ... I wish that we could see similar learnings going on in every classroom at every level."

JOANN B. LIPSHIRES
New Jersey Education Association

"Learning the Skills of Peacemaking addresses the problems of peace and negotiation precisely where the destinies of the superpowers are now being formulated—in the minds and souls of young people. The adoption of this remarkable educational program will surely be a positive force in international relations in years to come."

DAVID LANDAU
Author of *Kissinger: The Uses of Power*

"This peacemaking program will have an immediate impact on the lives of the children involved. Naomi Drew has not only articulated noble goals but has devised psychologically sound means to meet those goals."

BEATRICE GROSS
Author of *The Great School Debate: Which Way for American Education*

"The material is thoughtful, sensitive, and child-centered. It seems to me to be an intelligent, practical approach to a complex topic."

PROFESSOR VINCENT R. ROGERS
Dept. of Education, University of Connecticut

"How far we have come in peace education! Naomi Drew's book is packed full of exciting and usable new ideas and activities."

PRISCILLA PRUTZMAN
Author of *The Friendly Classroom for a Small Planet*

"Global peace begins with you. *Learning the Skills of Peacemaking* develops this fundamental concept in fifty-six lessons that personalize each individual's responsibility for respecting human differences, disavowing violence, and finding alternative means of resolving conflict. If this curriculum was a required course in every elementary school in every country, we would see world peace in our children's lifetime."

LETTY COTTIN POGREBIN
Author of *Family Politics, Growing Up Free,* and *Among Friends.* Also founding editor of *Ms.* magazine.

"There is a need to teach friendship and cooperation at the earliest level. My son has benefited from the understandings and concepts of this program."

MRS. SUSAN GRAZIANO
Parent of Student Participant

"Without question, your program is the most powerful I have ever participated in as an educator. You rekindled in me my purpose as a teacher to assist children in living in love and peace with themselves, their families, and friends and to take that attitude responsibly out into the world. Through your program, I have also experienced a sense of dignity as a teacher, which had been slowly falling away through the years."

GAIL WEITZ
Third Grade Teacher

"I am a strong advocate of Naomi Drew's curriculum, *Learning the Skills of Peacemaking*, because I know it works! As an educator and administrator, I see the effectiveness of the program and its positive impact by providing alternative methods of dealing with conflict within the schools. Discipline problems are greatly reduced, for students assume responsibility for their actions and take ownership of their feelings. Children learn cooperation, compromise, commitment, conflict resolution and other peacemaking skills. I highly recommend this program because it helps students become responsible, caring members of society."

LINDA M. COFFEY
Middle School Vice Principal

"Thank you, Naomi Drew for the gift of *Learning the Skills of Peacemaking*. After twenty years of teaching I have finally found a curriculum that gives substance to my work. Your book has helped me identify what had been in my heart for years: to teach my students, above anything else, to respect, support and affirm one another. Not only have my students started to help and encourage each other, they use the Win/Win Guidelines on their own to creatively resolve problems."

ROSEMARY PAPPA
Teacher/Consultant for Conflict Resolution

"*Learning the Skills of Peacemaking* has been critical in the creation of a peaceful, stimulating, successful learning environment for our students. Our teachers received training in peacemaking strategies and consistently implement the activities in the book. The Win/Win Guidelines are posted in every room in the school. Students and staff effectively resolve conflicts with dignity, confidence and mutual respect. Our students come to school secure in the knowledge that their rights are protected in a humane, systematic, effective manner. Graduates of our school are empowered to shape a more peaceful future because of this program."

MAURIE GRAFAS
Assistant Elementary Principal

"We have seen dramatic results in our school since embracing the principles and techniques espoused in Naomi Drew's book *Learning the Skills of Peacemaking*. Over the last two years we have reduced our discipline cases by nearly 70%. Kids *can* learn to resolve conflicts peacefully!"

GLENN FAMOUS
Elementary Principal

"I have used Naomi Drew's peacemaking guidelines for the past five years in my self-contained special education classes for learning disabled students. My students now feel empowered to resolve their own conflicts, without relying upon staff members. They realize their role in creating conflicts, and assume more responsibility for their actions and feelings. They grow to understand how their actions impact upon others, and such sensitivity allows for increased harmony in the classroom. This, in turn, provides an atmosphere that facilitates learning."

KAETRA M. HORTON, M.Ed., M.T.S.

"*Learning the Skills of Peacemaking* brings the skills of peacemaking to life in real situations. It's almost a bible for classroom management and, take it from us, it's really worth the small investment. ..."

TEACHING K-8, MAY 1988

"Naomi Drew has made a significant contribution to the knowledge and practice of peacemaking. Our teachers have found *Learning the Skills of Peacemaking* both inspiring and extremely constructive in the classroom. Naomi's ability to personally engage parents, students, and teachers in her instruction is unique."

SAMUEL B. STEWART
School Superintendent

"Would that I could be the peacemaker in your soul, that I might turn the discord and the rivalry of your elements into oneness and melody. But how shall I, unless you yourselves be also the peacemakers..."

Kahlil Gibran

SPECIAL THANKS

I'd like to thank the following people without whom the completion of this book and all of our work would not have been possible:

Michael Dee for enabling me to step out of the classroom and dedicate three years of my life to this work.

Marguerite Chandler for providing all of the many levels of support she has given to help this program grow and move forward.

Dr. Samuel H. McMillan, Jr., of the National Foundation for the Improvement of Education, for all his support and assistance.

Phyllis Yannetta for her loving, loyal, and continuous support, and for the hours of time she put into the preparation of this book.

Gail Weitz for her loving support and for the vital input she gave toward the shaping of new ideas for this book.

Jan Lovelady for her patience, support, and enthusiasm in the editing of this book.

Suzanne Mikesell for completing the editing of this book and for her thoughtful and perceptive comments.

Hal Sobel for his expert input as validator of the pilot program.

Bradley Winch, Sr., for his constant encouragement and helpfulness.

Therese LaMontagne for tirelessly typing the bulk of the manuscript.

My 1983-84 first grade class at the Clark Mills School in Manalapan-Englishtown who taught me more than they could ever imagine.

SPECIAL ACKNOWLEDGMENTS GO TO:

Heather Diaforli who created the beautiful painting that appears on the cover of this book.

AT&T, National Starch & Chemical, the Squibb Corporation, and the Edmar Corporation for providing grants to fund the pilot study.

The National Foundation for the Improvement of Education for their invaluable assistance in the research and development phase of this program.

I'd also like to acknowledge the following people as contributors to the lesson ideas in this book: Carole Messersmith, Pat Hoertdoerfer, Julia Greene, Judy Lepore, Gail Weitz, Linda Herman, and Priscilla Snow Algava.

Very special thanks to the Board of Partners in Peacemaking for their love, support, and enthusiasm:

Michael Dee, Bruce McCracken, Peter Jenkins, Andy Algava, Sandy Silverstone, Joana Reigel, Betty Levin, Richard Burke and Gail Weitz.

Thank you's for the revised edition of Learning the Skills of Peacemaking:

To my wonderful husband and sons for their constant love and support.

To Jeanne Iler, Susan Remkus, and Julia Tempel Olsen for their work on the new edition.

To Gail Siggelakis and Carol Lyons for their ideas and support.

To the South Brunswick District Conflict Resolution Committee for their ideas and input on peer mediation.

To all the boys and girls of Cambridge Elementary School who model the skills of peacemaking throughout the year.

This book is dedicated to: my two children, Michael and Tim Drew, whose lives have taught me to search for the meaning of peace for all human life,

and

to Norman Cousins, whose ideas and commitment to the "larger world" created the impetus for this book,

and

to my parents Molly and Philip Schreiber, without whom none of this would be possible.

CONTENTS

LEARNING THE SKILLS OF PEACEMAKING, Revised and Expanded

A K-6 ACTIVITY GUIDE ON RESOLVING CONFLICT, COMMUNICATING, COOPERATING

STAGE II: INTEGRATING PEACEMAKING INTO OUR LIVES

STAGE III: EXPLORING OUR ROOTS AND INTERCONNECTEDNESS

FOREWORD

At the core of this book is a simple but far-reaching idea: Peace can be achieved through individual effort and commitment to nonviolence. Peacemaking and conflict resolution techniques are not new concepts, but have emerged out of a necessity for solving global, institutional, and interpersonal disputes.

We have come to think of these resources as useful primarily to adults. *Learning the Skills of Peacemaking* demonstrates the importance of targeting our efforts toward another population: children. It is in childhood that our sense of self is born, our world view is formed, and our methods of dealing with frustration and conflict are learned. It is also during this time that our ideals are inspired. If as children we learn to be peaceful—optimistic that we can achieve our dreams—as adults we can spend our time contributing fully to society rather than undoing unproductive habits.

We know from research that the influence of the family on children's psychological and social development is great. Education, too, plays a key role in shaping children's attitudes. The classroom is a legitimate arena for engaging children in the process of peacemaking. In compiling this guide, Naomi Drew draws upon her experience as an educator, researcher, and parent. She provides concrete lesson plans and specific instruction in peacemaking techniques that foster self-respect, respect for others, and effective communication. She underscores the need to create a safe and nurturing learning environment that allows children to express their concerns and to arrive at creative and spontaneous solutions. Through understanding, flexibility, and negotiation, children learn to resolve problems assertively, without violence.

But the real challenge presented to educators and to us all is to become what we teach. The example that we set tells children more about how we really feel and think than words do. I am reminded here of a story in which a mother was discouraged because of her son's resistance to changing his poor eating habits. Knowing his admiration for Mahatma Gandhi she travelled 300 miles on foot with her son in the hope that Mahatma would counsel him not to eat sugar. When they arrived, Mahatma told them to return in two weeks. Despite her weariness and disappointment, she obeyed. Upon their return, Mahatma met with her son and it is said that out of devotion to this great leader, the child changed his ways. The mother, however, asked Mahatma why he chose not to speak with her son on the first visit. It is said that Mahatma replied, "Two weeks ago I was eating sugar."

As children begin to understand and integrate peacemaking techniques, it then becomes appropriate to extend these lessons to address global issues. Children are given the opportunity to explore the similarities and differences in customs, attitudes, and policies of other nations and to believe in a possibility of a world at peace. Through clarity about our goal and perseverance in our commitment to effect peace, we can dispel the discouragement that comes from the belief that violence and war are inevitable. As we begin to disseminate information on innovative and peaceful approaches to conflict resolution and to share our knowledge, we will make the great longing for world peace a reality.

Learning the Skills of Peacemaking is an integral part of this process.

Yogesh K. Gandhi, Founder, Gandhi Memorial International Foundation

THE LIGHT-BEARERS

by Jessica Hirst, age 11

Light, cascading down
Turning rainbow colors
Over, under, through almost everything
Obstructions are overcome
Light washes over beings
Some greedily take it in
And keep it for their own pleasure
Many try to use it positively, help it grow
They try, but they do not have the knowledge
A few accept it, have knowledge to use it
They teach others
These few are the Light-Bearers
To carry the light for others
To give Light to beings
A sad child
A despairing youth
A weary elder
All are taught
The sun will rise again
Have hope, hold it tight
Be Light-Bearers
Help hurt ones, before souls flee
Overcome selfishness, cruelty
Save yourselves from self-destruction
Light, cascading down
Turning rainbow colors
Into the welcoming arms
Of the Light-Bearers

PREFACE

If we are to reach real peace in the world we shall have to begin with children; and if they will grow up in their natural innocence, we won't have to struggle; we won't have to pass fruitless ideal resolutions, but we shall go from love to love and peace to peace, until at last all the corners of the world are covered with that peace and love for which consciously or unconsciously the whole world is hungering.

Gandhi

During the first eleven years that I taught elementary school, I came to realize that the system educates children about reading, language, math, and other subjects, but not about the most important one of all: how to interact with each other and the world at large. I began to research the issues that most concern today's children, and what I found was that young people have deep fears about the future. They are very much affected by the violence surrounding them.

I also learned that when students are given a chance to discuss the future, a future free of violence and how they might help bring about such a future, they become more hopeful. They begin to see the possibility of a role for themselves in creating a peaceful future.

I felt a strong need for a program that would actually teach the skills of peacemaking in the same way math, reading, and spelling are taught. Such a program would demonstrate that peacemaking, like math or reading, is logical, practical, invaluable.

I expanded the program I first piloted in my own school over the years and it is now used by schools and communities in many different states and in a variety of different countries. In fact, the program has gained so much recognition that it was presented to members of the White House staff in 1986.

What began it all was an in-depth examination of the following questions:

- How does education prepare young people for the future when so many feel their future is at risk?

- Does education offer youth values and a sense of responsibility to the world beyond themselves, or simply training in basic skills?

- Does education offer children good reasons to live and hope?

- Are young people learning the skills they'll need to deal with a rapidly changing technology and an expanding concept of the world?

- Does education empower youth to begin shaping the future? If not, how can it begin to do this?

Learning the Skills of Peacemaking addresses these questions. It teaches specific skills as well as a general problem-solving process by which children can begin to create the kind of future we all want: a peaceful one. It demonstrates that cooperation is not only achievable at home and at school, it may actually be more natural for us than conflict. Conflict, while always present in life, does not need to determine its course. Generally, we prefer to get along with each other, to work out our differences.

Ask your students or your children which kind of atmosphere they prefer—one of anger and upset, or one of peacefulness and harmony? The choice is evident. We prefer harmony, but we are not always sure how to achieve it. Creating an atmosphere of acceptance and peace is possible, but maintaining it takes enormous commitment, practice, and the willingness to leave old habits behind. Choosing conciliation over opposition is a constant challenge.

An atmosphere of peacefulness and compromise includes the following elements:

- cooperation

- calmness

- willingness to work out differences

- ability to work collaboratively to solve problems

- love and acceptance

- the ability to say, "I'm human. I've made a mistake. I'll try again."

An atmosphere of peacefulness supports the well-being of all parties involved. It's a dynamic atmosphere in which the old ways are questioned as the new ways evolve.

Peace begins with the individual commitment to having a better world. Education can foster this commitment. You, as the teacher, are able to take the first step in imparting this dynamic. Your way of dealing with discipline, resolving conflicts, affirming each child's value, and pointing out his or her connections to the world forms the base for a commitment to peace.

Learning the Skills of Peacemaking was designed to be used as a springboard for positive interactions with your students. Integrate the texture of each lesson into the classroom atmosphere. By using the techniques in this book throughout the day, you will create a calm, cooperative, peaceful classroom.

Peace is more than the absence of war. It is an active, collaborative process by which human beings take direct responsibility for dealing with the problems they face. It is the key to the future.

Naomi Drew
1995

HOW THIS BOOK CAME TO BE

Nothing is more important than an individual acting out of his conscience, thus helping to bring the collective conscience to life.

Norman Cousins

I came to a point in my life when I knew I had something important to express, create, contribute. Not yet knowing what it would be, I searched for a vehicle that would spark a nerve deep inside me. That vehicle turned out to be the book *Human Options* by Norman Cousins. When I read it the effect was no less potent than a tidal wave sweeping me up in its momentum.

That was 1982. The issue of nuclear weapons was in the papers daily, and reading about it made me think of what could happen if there was ever a nuclear war. I worried about the people I most loved: my family, my friends, and the children I taught. Around that same time, I started hearing praise for Cousins' book, touted for bringing to light the idea that although we lived in a time of potential nuclear crisis, we all had the potential to shape the future through our involvement. It focused on the vital role of individual action. Individual action—the nerve was being sparked.

I rushed to the bookstore as soon as *Human Options* came out. As I held the book in my hands, I remember the distinct visceral feeling that it would change my life. I began reading it, and the profound nature of Cousins' words inspired and moved me:

> *The starting point for a better world is the belief that it is possible. Civilization begins in the imagination. The wild dream is the first step to reality. It is the direction-finder by which people locate higher goals and discern their highest selves.*
> (Cousins 52)

Highest self. What was the mission of my highest self? I pondered this, and it was as though the question was reaching inside me, groping toward some indefinable part that had lain dormant. The momentum was starting and I knew I had to translate this powerful question into some kind of action. Not knowing what else to do, I decided to write Norman Cousins. I opened my heart to him, expressing the sense of helplessness I felt at being the mother of two young children when the future of all children seemed so tenuous. I spoke of wanting to make a difference, a contribution to the world we lived in. Several weeks later I received a reply in which Cousins said, "As long as there are people like you who care, there is hope for the future." Although his words touched me, they threw me into a quandary. What could I do—a suburban mother, wife, and teacher?

"The mission of the highest self." The words kept pulling at me as I struggled with the question: What can I do as a teacher to impact the future? After a lot of reading, soul-searching, and talking to other people, I came across these words of Gandhi: "If we are able to reach real peace in the world we shall have to begin with the children." Gandhi's words forced me to ask myself: How can I plant the seeds of peace in the young minds of my students? The dormant part of me was coming to life; the mission I was striving toward was finally starting to define itself. It was clear that I would "begin with children." What better time than in the earliest years of learning, when minds were still open and fresh?

This insight became the embryo of this book, which started as a guide for my first grade class. This book has brought me to the White House, to Russia, and to workshops throughout the country as a presenter.

How did the seed grow into something so far-reaching, something still growing and touching more lives than I had ever anticipated? Cousins' idea that individuals could change society lit a fire inside me. I was moved to step beyond the confines of my ordinary life to achieve something larger.

I began putting together a curriculum that embodied Cousins' concept of a shared world where people took responsibility for the greater harmony. The first time I talked with my students about peacemaking I tried to convey all of the feeling that was motivating my new direction. Choked with emotion, I found it difficult to speak.

"Boys and girls," I started nervously as we sat in our circle on the floor, "I care so much about you. Sometimes I look at the world we live in and worry about the future for all of us. We know of so many instances where people hurt each other, countries hurt each other. There's got to be something we can do now, while you're little, to start changing things."

I paused and looked at my children. Their eyes shone with concern and care, giving me the courage to go on. "I've been thinking about ways we can do our small part in creating a better world, a world where people show respect and live together peacefully. Perhaps if we can start here, other people will be able to do it too. Would you like to work on this together?"

The children were visibly moved. There was a chorus of nods amid the reverent silence. Mark raised his hand and said, "Yes, Mrs. Drew. But what can we do?"

At this point I showed them a globe, explaining that it represented the world we lived in, a world we shared with other people. I said, "All human beings share this earth together. In order to live peacefully, we need to find ways to work out our differences without hurting each other. That's the place to start."

We began talking about how crucial it was for people to get along and accept differences. We spoke about the need everyone had for love, care, respect, and how the responsibility for treating each other humanely rested with each individual. The children acknowledged their understanding

of all this, especially the importance of trying to find ways to resolve conflicts nonviolently.

Every morning after that, we would sit in our circle on the floor and talk about ways we could be peacemakers in school, at home, and in life. I started introducing conflict resolution guidelines, and the children began sharing stories of how they were trying to work out their problems with friends and family members instead of fighting.

Gradual changes in my students started surfacing. With each daily discussion, I noticed a growing sensitivity. They began listening more intently to one another, speaking kinder words, and using the "I Messages" I had taught them to state their problems. As each day went by, there was a greater degree of respect among all of them. A sense of peace began to permeate the classroom.

People who came into the classroom commented on the harmony that seemed to be ever-present. Parents, administrators and other teachers wanted to know what I was doing to bring about these changes. One child's mother told me that her son's Sunday school teacher had asked her what we were doing in school, saying, "Michael has begun to show an added sensitivity that is very unusual in children his age." Michael's mom told him about the "peacemaking program," as we had begun to call it. The parents of many of my students asked me to show them how to use our "Win/Win" conflict resolution guidelines.

After six months I decided it was time to share with other teachers what I was doing.

I led my first workshop through the New Jersey Education Association and I was so nervous my knees shook (although the participants didn't seem to notice). The response was excellent, and it became obvious this would become the first of many workshops. The "highest self" that had once lain dormant was beginning to reach out toward a larger audience.

By summer, I had an eighty page peacemaking guide completed and knew it needed to be shared beyond the walls of my classroom. The vision begun with *Human Options* was coming to life. People at NJEA directed me to a foundation in Washington called the National Foundation for the

Improvement of Education, dedicated to finding and nationally disseminating exemplary educational programs. Fueled by possibility but not expecting much, I sent a copy of the guide to the director. The following week I got a call from Washington. It was the director of the National Foundation asking me to come to Washington! I was elated and in a state of disbelief. Could this really be happening?

When I arrived in Washington, the reaction of the director floored me. His words are imprinted on my memory: "This is one of the finest programs I have ever seen. It should be used in schools throughout the country. The National Foundation would like to make that possible." I had never expected such a response to the program that I had been doing with my students in our circle each morning. I rushed to call my family, and I couldn't wait to tell my class. I was doing it. I was really doing it!

That was the beginning. I ended up taking a leave of absence from my teaching job to work on the program, plunging into the hardest and most exhilarating two and a half years of my life. One of the greatest challenges was in raising my two boys alone while we struggled to survive on grant monies, never knowing if the next grant would be awarded. There were many nights I would wake up in a panic, thinking, What am I doing? How could I have left a secure teaching job to jump into a venture that may never come to fruition? Having put our financial stability at stake was scary and risky, but I refused to be deterred from my goal.

Learning the Skills of Peacemaking became a reality in October of 1986, four years after I had read *Human Options.* When I held my own book in my hands it was the most unbelievable feeling in the world, almost equal to the birth of my children.

It's been nine years since this book was released, and it's now in its ninth printing. I know from the letters and phone calls I have received from people around the country and beyond that my book is touching lives. Recently, I received a letter from an eight-year-old girl named Rachel. She said, "Thank you for writing the peacemaking book. It has really changed my life. It has helped me at school and at home. I love peacemaking. I wish it was all

over the world." This sentiment has been echoed by the teachers, parents, and students who have reached out to me over the years. It seemed that I had come full-circle.

As soon as my book came out, I sent a copy of it to Norman Cousins. His quote, which now appears on the back cover, reminds me of how one life can touch another, moving a powerful idea from hand to hand, heart to heart, creating change in the process. He said:

> *I am deeply touched that my book* Human Options *figured in your decision to create* Learning the Skills of Peacemaking, *and I offer you every good wish with this important undertaking.*

In deciding to commit myself to an idea much larger than anything I had experienced before, and seeing the idea through its many stages to completion, I have finally come to understand what Norman Cousins meant when he talked about the power of the individual acting out of one's conscience, "…thus helping to bring the collective conscience to life."

I hope my book will do for you what Norman Cousins' book did for me.

INTRODUCTION

Learning the Skills of Peacemaking is a guide for teachers, parents, and other caregivers who wish to bring the skills of peacemaking to life for children. It focuses on four major concepts:

- Accepting self and others
- Communicating effectively
- Resolving conflicts
- Understanding intercultural differences

Peacemaking skills are presented in three "stages," with each stage integrating lessons in these four concept areas. There are fifty-nine lessons in all. Stage I is "Peace Begins with Me," Stage II is "Integrating Peacemaking," and Stage III is "Exploring Our Roots and Interconnectedness." Each stage is multigraded. Although I recommend some of the lessons for particular grade levels, please adapt them to your own class situation even if your students don't fall into the suggested grade level range.

Peruse the entire guide before you begin to teach it, to see which lessons best suit your classroom needs. Each class is different. Your creativity and flexibility in the use of this book will make it more meaningful to your children. Don't be afraid to do the lessons in a different order, either. Just make sure to introduce any new ideas or terminology carefully. Some of the concepts will be completely new to your students.

Learning the Skills of Peacemaking uses many methods to teach peacemaking skills, such as: playacting, creative writing, story-reading, music, the arts, and classroom discussion. The lessons can be used approximately twice a week to enrich other areas of your curriculum. See page 11 for a complete content integration chart. However, since the concepts and values in each lesson are meant to be woven into all your daily interactions, use them regularly throughout the week to fully nurture a classroom atmosphere of peacemaking.

For example, you can use the deep breathing technique first thing in the morning to set a calm tone for the day. The conflict resolution guidelines can be applied whenever a stressful situation arises. "Showcase" conflict situations as they occur, mediating them through the use of the Win/Win Guidelines, and engage the entire class in problem solving (see the next chapter for a discussion of The Win/Win Guidelines and the concept of "showcasing.") Occasionally stopping whatever you are doing to resolve a conflict and explaining that this is part of the process of peacemaking can have a tremendous impact.

Remember, the basic concepts in *Learning the Skills of Peacemaking* are interwoven in each stage. As the children focus on peacemaking in their lives, they begin to see how these skills can be applied to the world beyond themselves. Thus the lessons become more abstract as they go along.

You will find current events infused into each section to highlight the connection between individual acts and world events. For example, at one point when the children are learning conflict resolution skills, they examine a selected current event article relating to a conflict situation. They are asked: "How can this situation be resolved through the use of conflict resolution skills?" Such a query broadens their perspective and guides them to recognize that they are a part of the larger world—community, nation, and earth—as well as of the smaller one—home, neighborhood, and school.

Children discover that they belong to the whole human family, that they are connected in many ways to other people throughout the world. More importantly, they learn that peace begins with each person, that the same techniques that average people use to work out problems can be used by world leaders. This is not to over-simplify the complexities of today's international conflicts, but to show that individuals, regardless of title or position, have options they can pursue to resolve differences.

MAKING PARENTS YOUR PARTNERS

When I first started developing the peacemaking lessons in my 1983-84 first grade class, parents of my students became curious. I began receiving calls, like this one from Todd's mother: "Mrs. Drew, what are you doing with Todd? He's started acting differently. He seems to be more willing to work out problems and he's not fighting with his brother as much. When I asked him why the sudden change, he said, 'We're learning how to be peacemakers in our school. Our teacher's showing us ways we can get along better.' Could you tell me about what you're doing? I'd like to learn it, too."

Another mom said: "Michelle's soccer coach said that she has developed strategies to work out conflicts with other children. He asked me what I was doing to bring this about. I told him that Michelle was doing a special program in school. Could you tell me more about it?"

After several conversations, I invited the parents to come in and observe or participate in lessons. I also held some after-school meetings. This was effective on several levels: it helped create a greater partnership with the parents; it provided hands-on information and techniques; and it enabled parents to understand what we were doing in school so they could reinforce the ideas at home.

Holding meetings for parents will help you build a partnership with them. September is a good time to begin. An after-school coffee or an evening meeting will provide the opportunity to

show them this guide and introduce its concepts and goals. A visual display such as the "Me Mobiles" from Lesson 4 is a great conversation piece. Parents always enjoy seeing their children's work displayed, especially projects of such a personal nature as the mobiles.

A step beyond observation is to actually include parents in some of the lessons. Many lessons lend themselves to "audiences," oral report presentations in particular. Any opportunity to involve parents supports their efforts to reinforce at home the skills their children are learning at school.

THE HIERARCHY OF PEACEMAKING

Think of yourself as holding up a tall ladder. You are at the base. If you let go, the ladder topples. If your grip is firm, the ladder is steady. So it is with peacemaking. Peace starts with each individual. It emerges first from within and then manifests itself most basically in the way people feel about themselves. I reiterate the importance of a positive self-concept in this book because this is the critical key to becoming a successful peacemaker. Self-concept influences our every action, interaction, and reaction.

With a positive self-image, you are ready to go up to the next rung on the ladder—one-to-one interactions. This level encompasses interpersonal relationships—those between friends, teacher and student, brother and sister, neighbors, etc. At this place on the ladder we challenge students to communicate effectively, resolve conflicts positively, and solve problems collaboratively.

Relationships in small groups follow—family, neighborhood, school, religious groups, civic groups, etc. Peacemaking moves up to encompass greater numbers of people and more complex interactions. Shifting for a moment to look back, down to the source, become aware that it is the inner landscape that largely determines how you will relate in groups. When you feel whole and at peace within, you can relate to others more effectively. When you feel unworthy, inadequate, or troubled, you will manifest such emotions in the way you deal with and perceive others. Think about the children in your class. Almost inevitably those who act out or are withdrawn from others are children who don't feel good about themselves.

As you continue to move up the ladder, you encounter larger and larger groups. You step up to the community, then the state, the nation, the hemisphere, and finally the world. How you perceive and relate to the world depends on how you relate to yourself. Ask yourself:

- How can I serve the world beyond myself?

- How can I best relate to the people around me?

- How can I reach out beyond what looks like my small sphere of influence into a larger sphere?

- How can I make a difference in the world?

REPEATING THE LESSONS

Just as number facts need to be reviewed periodically, so it is with peacemaking skills. These lessons are designed to be repeated year after year, with variations supplied by each teacher. If you are teaching third grade, for example, and your class did most of the peacemaking lessons in second grade, I would suggest doing the lessons again but modifying them in your own way. Have a class discussion. Tell the children that because their growth and experiences during the past year provided them with new insights and understandings, their present responses to the lessons will be somewhat different. Let the children know that repeating lessons reinforces their changing attitudes and behaviors.

You will need to be creative in this effort. You can vary the activities and discussions but keep the objectives in mind when doing so. Brainstorm with other teachers and find out what new ideas they've discovered in teaching peacemaking skills. I would be delighted to see any new activities and lessons you come up with.

Remember, repetition is critical to a child's absorption of new understandings. Change takes time, practice, and adaptation, but it should be enjoyable, too. Making the lessons fun will enhance your children's grasp of the material.

THE IMPORTANCE OF TEACHING PEACEMAKING SKILLS

I have discovered that inevitably something starts to "shift" as teachers and children internalize the concepts of peacemaking presented in this book. Here is an example shared by one teacher:

"The room was so quiet you could hear your own breathing. The children were seated on the floor in a circle, legs crossed. Each child was deep in thought. The children were asked to imagine the world just as they would want it to be. They were asked to imagine people of all races, religions, colors, and nationalities getting along. How would the world look? How would it be different from the way it is now? How would they feel if the world were this way?

"The children sat for a few moments in deep concentration and silence. One by one they began to speak. One boy said, 'I pictured black and white children playing together.' A little girl said, 'I pictured a world with no more wars, where people learned to work out their differences together.' "

Be aware that children, as well as adults, may resist the shift toward peacemaking in a non-peaceful world. Some teachers have said,

"Sometimes children come to me and say, 'I'm not a peacemaker because there are times I still fight,' or, 'Why should I try to get along with others, when they don't try to get along with me?' " Expect such questions—they are part of the process of integrating peacemaking skills. You will challenge children's perceptions as well as their actions in this program, and change takes time.

Be patient and be aware of the small, gradual changes as they evolve. As one teacher said after completing *Learning the Skills of Peacemaking*, "Some of my children still fight, but now they've begun to take responsibility for their actions."

USING THIS GUIDE: NOTES FOR TEACHERS AND PARENTS

Although parents as well as teachers will be using this guide, I refer to "classroom" and "students" rather than "family" and "children" for simplicity's sake. Please adapt the instructions for your use with individuals or groups, as appropriate.

BEGIN WITH A DISCUSSION:

Tell the class about your own commitment to having a peaceful class. Give your reasons for caring about this. Discuss them with the group. Discuss students' feelings and responses, along the following lines:

"What kind of classroom atmosphere do you want to have?"

"How do you want to be treated by your classmates?"

"What do you think are the qualities of a peaceful class?"

Make a preliminary chart of the qualities and hang it up. Use it as a beginning, a starting point. The list of qualities will grow. Have each class member participate in the completion of this chart. Review it together from time to time to reinforce the concepts. Complete your discussion with the following questions:

- "How would our class be if we all did our very best to get along?"

- "How would the world be different if everybody were committed to peace and knew how to make it a reality?"

- What does it mean when we say, "Peace begins with you"?

Don't be surprised if your students voice feelings of despair, resignation, or apathy during the discussion. Allow this to happen and allow your own negative feelings to surface as well. This is a crucial part of the process. As you become more and more involved in peacemaking, you'll begin to recognize the unworkability of old patterns or solutions. Sometimes this is manifested as a lack of faith in new solutions.

For instance, you might think "This can't work. Human nature just isn't conducive to putting aside differences and agreeably resolving conflict." If this happens, know that the reverse side of this feeling is a feeling of possibility. Giving in to hopelessness renders us powerless. Your faith in the process is the catalyst—through it you will discover that slowly you can develop harmony and cooperation in school and at home. *It takes time.* Remember this, and be patient.

Daily interactions are usually the first demonstration of one's commitment to peace. In my own family, we had an extended discussion about this. One of the questions that came up was, "How can we expect nations to get along if we can't get along in our own home?" The realization that followed was, if we could find ways to work out differences and get along in our own home, then perhaps other people could do it, too. We talked about the fact that people hurt each other all the time throughout the world, but if we wanted a better, safer world, then it had to first start at home.

My children began to see that we all must take responsibility for peacemaking. Often it's much easier to place the blame for conflict on others or on circumstances. Looking within and discovering our own responsibility in each conflict goes against many ingrained behaviors. But that's precisely where authentic problem-solving and peacemaking begin.

Bringing forth your students' belief and commitment before teaching the conflict resolution process is extremely important. Vision and commitment are the most vital elements in any peacemaking effort. Without them, the process is hollow and meaningless. *A commitment is a promise we make to ourselves and others—that we keep no matter what.* It's not based on circumstances; it does not depend on the actions of others. A commitment is rooted within each person and is entirely dependent upon his or her willingness to generate it.

Ask your children, "Are you willing to be committed to working out your differences with other people?" Talk this over and let them know that sometimes we have to take the first step in conflict resolution ourselves. Now ask: "What would it be like if people all over the world, including leaders of government, were committed first and foremost to working out differences nonviolently?"

If you find yourself reacting negatively right now, ask yourself, Do you believe peace is possible? Take a moment to think about this now. What would the world be like if it were completely at peace? Imagine the details. What did you come up with? Can you believe in the possibility of a world at peace, or is something in the way? If so, what is it? Talk about this with others. The belief is the source as well as the goal. Taking steps to incorporate the skills of peacemaking into your life begins with a belief that peace is possible. The goal or destination is the realization of the belief. The whole process starts with you, as an individual.

Reflect for a moment on the possibility that global peace may begin with you and the actions you choose during each moment of your life.

CLASS (OR FAMILY) MEETINGS:

There are different ways to create an atmosphere of peace in the school and home. The class or family meeting helps you to set the context for cooperation. If you set the tone through discussions, you'll find it easier to establish mutual agreements to solve problems. If possible, have a class or family meeting at least once a week at a set time. In the classroom, sitting in a circle on the floor or in chairs works best. This creates a sense of equal partnership—no one's in the front or back of the room—and also a feeling of connectedness. In the home, the best place to hold meetings is at the kitchen table. When young children are involved, the teacher or parent can run the meetings. Alternate this leadership role with older children.

Rules for meetings might be:

- The goal is to improve the atmosphere in the class or home, not to rehash differences or "dump."
- Each person gets a turn to speak.
- There are no interruptions.
- Each person must agree not to make negative comments about any other person.
- Each person must listen to the speaker.
- Each person must agree to consider things from the speaker's perspective rather than focusing only on his own thoughts.

Write down any group decisions or agreements—ones that are based upon full class or family discussion and participation—and post them where they can easily be seen. As the meeting goes along, the facilitator may want to thank each person who expresses an opinion or idea; this acknowledges participation and encourages those who might tend to be reticent.

Class or family meetings provide the opportunity for airing differences, resolving problems, and working together cooperatively. Children enjoy being included in the decision-making process—it helps them become more autonomous and responsible. Also, the sense of the class or family as a unit emerges out of this kind of participation.

DISCIPLINING WITH LOVE: SOME GUIDELINES

Utilize the following guidelines to enhance your ability to nurture peaceful behaviors:

1. *Remember that you are capable of reaching each child.*

Studies prove that children from classes (families) in which their teachers (parents) believe in them and expect them to succeed, generally do succeed. Where academic expectations are negative, negative performance follows. So it is with behavior. When you expect the negative, you get it. When you know that each child is capable of behaving and cooperating, and when you act on this belief, you evoke positive behaviors. You will drastically reduce the need for disciplinary measures by focusing on and expecting the positive.

2. *Affirmation*

An affirmation is a sincere compliment we give to another person. The more you affirm your children, the better. When we affirm, we're holding up a mirror to the other person through which they can see the best in themselves. Every affirmation is a gift. Give this gift often and freely. It will always be returned.

3. *Catch children in the act of doing something right and acknowledge them immediately.*

This guideline doesn't mean ignoring negative behavior but rather shifting the focus from negative to positive attention. It works. Try it. You can also start by making a list of all the positive attributes of the child who is giving you the most difficulty. Share this list with the child to support his or her self-image. Each time you see that child engaged in a positive behavior, acknowledge him or her for it. You can add to the list daily as well. Keep doing this and see what happens.

Catching your students in the act of "doing it right":
The class is noisy. You want the children to settle down for the next lesson. You state: "Boys and girls I'd like you to settle down, take out your math books, and show me you're ready to begin the lesson." The majority of the class continues to talk. Five children are following your direction. You state: "Kathy, I like the way you're taking out your math book and getting ready for the lesson. You're sitting quietly, too. Thanks. Eric, you're also following directions really well. You're ready for the lesson. Your pencils and eraser are out and your book is already open to the correct page. That's great."

You will begin to notice that each time you sincerely acknowledge positive behaviors, others in the class will begin to follow. As this happens, give a brief acknowledgment to each child: "Terry, you're ready too. Great." And so on until the class has become quiet and attentive, at which time you can acknowledge them as a group. Children love to be noticed. If they can't draw your attention with positive behaviors, they'll try the opposite. Everyone wins when the focus is on the positive.

Catching your children in the act of "doing it right" at home:

Your children are playing a game. Two of them are arguing and annoying each other. The third is playing quietly, not participating in the argument. You might say: "Jess, I like the way you've been playing cooperatively. You're being considerate of your brothers. Thanks." Notice what the others do when you react this way: More than likely, they'll follow the positive lead when you acknowledge (affirm) the one acting positively. It's not necessary to call attention to the negative behaviors. Haim Ginott brilliantly describes this process in *Teacher & Child*[1]—a must read for anyone who wants to create a positive learning/living environment.

If the negative behaviors continue, you have several alternatives:

Give Choices: "Jason and Carl, you can either stop arguing or put the game away."

Make a Request: "I'd like to ask you to play quietly now. It disturbs me to see you arguing. Are you willing to stop arguing and continue your game?"

Time Out: "It seems to me that you boys need a break from one another. Jason, you sit at the kitchen table for a while. Carl, you sit on the couch. When you feel ready to resume playing calmly you can return to the game."

Apply the Win/Win Guidelines (see page 17).

NOTE: I strongly urge you to pick up a copy of *Parent Effectiveness Training* by Thomas Gordon[2] or *Effectiveness Training for Women* (great for men, too) by Linda Adams[3]. These books provide excellent background on the use of effective listening tools and "I messages," which you will need if you have no such prior experience. Keep a copy of one or both of these references in your classroom or home.

Notice that none of the above techniques passes judgment or levies a punishment. This is not to say that punishment is never appropriate. When all else has failed, punishment may be the next step. Just remember, if you punish, avoid name calling, judging, or moralizing. Simply address the behavior you want changed and state your feeling about it.

Example:

"Now I'm angry, Jason and Carl. I've asked you to stop arguing and you've chosen to continue anyway. I'm losing my patience and I want you to go to your rooms."

Notice the difference between this interaction and the following:

(Name Calling): "Jason and Carl, you're a couple of pests and you're driving me crazy."

(Judging): "What a naughty thing to do! You deserve to be punished because you're being so bad."

(Moralizing): "If you were good boys you would stop fighting when I ask you to. When I was little I always listened to my mother."

The parent in the first example allowed her children to understand her position without making them feel attacked. When people feel attacked, they don't want to cooperate.

There is a form of creative punishment that you might wish to try called "conditional punishment," in which a privilege is revoked but the child is given the opportunity to earn it back through positive behavior.

Example:

"Okay, Jason and Carl. You've had the chance to work out your differences, but you're not cooperating. Tonight you won't be able to watch TV. However, there is a way you can earn back the privilege. If you can play the game together without annoying one another, I'll consider allowing you to earn back the privilege to watch one show this evening."

4. *Use reward systems.*

Make a chart. Write down behaviors you want the particular child to accomplish. Have the child meet with you each morning and at the end of the day to review the goals set out on the chart and the progress made. This can be done at school and/or at home.

The following format can be used:

Tim's Star Chart	Mon.	Tue.	Wed.	Thur.	Fri.
I completed my classwork.					
I finished my homework.					
I get along with the children sitting next to me.					
I did neat and careful work.					
I paid attention in class.					

Each time the child accomplishes the indicated behavior, put a star on the chart. If you're doing this in school, at the end of each week write a note to the child's parents indicating how many goals were accomplished. Don't use the chart for negative reinforcement by stressing goals not accomplished. Praise the child for what he/she achieved, and be specific about it. For example, "Tim, you completed all your homework as well as your classwork today. Everything was neat and carefully done. Congratulations." This type of praise is much more effective than, "You did good work." After the child has been steadily accomplishing his or her goals, start to phase out the chart so it doesn't become a crutch.

5. *Express lots of love.*

The more you focus on loving feelings, the less room there will be for negative ones. Think of yourself as a radio with lots of adjustable dials. You can "fine-tune" your listening so your radio picks up that which is positive about a particular child. Keep noticing the good points. In fact, make that list of attributes we talked about before. Keep expanding the list each time you notice a new one. Share the list with the child, and let him/her feel acknowledged.

6. *Be kind to yourself.*

In today's busy society, we sometimes inflict a subtle form of violence upon ourselves called stress. This comes about through pressure, over-work, and excessive expectations. When you are tense and burdened, it's hard to act in a loving way. In his book, *One Minute for Myself,* Spencer

Johnson suggests taking a minute several times a day and asking, "Is there a way for me to take better care of myself right now?"[4] Try it—you may begin to feel less pressured and thus more relaxed with others. In treating yourself lovingly, you spread the positive feeling to those around you. If you're a teacher, see if you and another teacher (or teachers) can support each other in being good to yourselves. Little things count—a walk together at lunch time, a quiet moment together after school where you can let your hair down.

7. *Have fun together.*

As a teacher or parent, planning "fun" into your days is important. Light, relaxing, joyful, or silly activities can take the edge off a busy day. Five minutes of fun can spark energy and create a more alive atmosphere wherever you might be. Imagine laughter as the antidote to deprivation of the spirit. When we allow ourselves to experience the joy of human interconnectedness, our relationships flourish. Plan at least one fun activity each day, even if it is only for a few minutes. You will notice the difference this makes for you as well as the children.

Footnotes:
[1] Ginott, Haim, *Teacher & Child*, New York: MacMillan, 1972.
[2] Gordon, Thomas, *Parent Effectiveness Training*, New York: Peter Weyden, 1970.
[3] Adams, Linda, *Effectiveness Training for Women*, New York: Weyden Books, 1979.
[4] Johnson, Spencer, *One Minute for Myself*, New York: Weyden Books, 1979.

INTEGRATING *LEARNING THE SKILLS OF PEACEMAKING* INTO OTHER CONTENT AREAS

Here's how the lessons in this book tie into other parts of your curriculum.

Lesson Number and Title	Grade Level	Social Studies	Language Arts	Values	Well-being	Thinking Skills	Art
Stage I							
1. Creating a Peaceful Classroom	ALL	✔	✔	✔	✔	✔	
2. Resolving Conflicts: The Quick Method	K - 2	✔	✔	✔	✔	✔	
3. Resolving Conflicts: The Quick Method	3 - 6	✔	✔	✔	✔	✔	
4. I'm a Special and Unique Person	ALL	✔	✔		✔		✔
5. Defining Peace	ALL	✔	✔	✔	✔	✔	✔
6. The Process of Affirming	ALL	✔	✔	✔	✔		✔
7. Defining Conflict Resolution	ALL	✔	✔		✔	✔	
8. What Gets in the Way of Resolving Conflicts	ALL	✔	✔	✔	✔	✔	
9. Using "I Messages"	ALL	✔	✔		✔	✔	
10. Win/Win Guidelines	ALL	✔	✔	✔	✔	✔	
11. What Else Can I Do?	1 - 6	✔	✔		✔	✔	
12. Reflective Listening	ALL	✔	✔	✔	✔	✔	✔
13. Cooperative Group Simulations	2 - 6	✔	✔	✔		✔	
14. Creative Brainstorming	ALL	✔	✔	✔		✔	
15. Brainstorming Solutions to Conflicts	ALL	✔	✔	✔		✔	
16. Taking Care of Our Earth	ALL	✔	✔	✔		✔	
17. Taking Care of People in Our Community	ALL	✔	✔	✔		✔	
18. Taking Care of Those Who Are Hungry	ALL	✔	✔	✔		✔	
19. The Basic Needs of People	ALL	✔	✔	✔		✔	
20. We Are All Interconnected	ALL	✔	✔	✔		✔	

Lesson Number and Title	Grade Level	Social Studies	Language Arts	Values	Well-being	Thinking Skills	Art
Stage I (con't)							
21. What is a Peacemaker	ALL	✔	✔	✔		✔	
22. Things I'm Good At	ALL	✔	✔		✔		✔
23. Using Peacemaking Logs	ALL	✔	✔		✔	✔	
24. Peacemaking Logs: Feeling Special	ALL	✔	✔		✔	✔	
25. Peacemaker of the Week	ALL	✔	✔	✔		✔	
26. Peacemakers in My Life	ALL	✔	✔	✔		✔	
Stage II 27. Peace Starts with Me	ALL	✔	✔	✔	✔	✔	✔
28. Making Ethical Choices I	1 - 6	✔	✔	✔	✔	✔	
29. Making Ethical Choices II	2 - 6	✔	✔	✔	✔	✔	
30. Making Ethical Choices III	3 - 6	✔	✔	✔	✔	✔	
31. Making Ethical Choices IV	3 - 6	✔	✔	✔	✔	✔	
32. Connecting to the World Around Us	1 - 6	✔	✔	✔	✔		
33. Our Visions are Special	ALL	✔	✔		✔	✔	✔
34. Our Vision of a Peaceful School	ALL	✔	✔		✔	✔	✔
35. The Nicest Thing About	ALL	✔	✔	✔	✔	✔	✔
36. Being Different is OK	ALL	✔	✔	✔			✔
37. Other People Are Different Too	ALL	✔	✔	✔			✔
38. Our Feelings are OK	ALL	✔	✔	✔	✔	✔	✔
39. My Friend is Different and He/She is Special	ALL	✔	✔	✔			✔
40. Human Differences: Being Jaime	ALL	✔	✔	✔			✔
41. Different Flags of Different Lands	2 - 6	✔	✔				✔
42. Different Flags: Oral Reports	2 - 6	✔	✔				

Lesson Number and Title	Grade Level	Social Studies	Language Arts	Values	Well-being	Thinking Skills	Art
Stage II (con't)							
43. Taking Part in Our Communities	ALL	✔	✔	✔		✔	
44. Sentence Writing Using Familiar Terms	2 - 6	✔	✔				
45. Conflicts in the News	2 - 6	✔	✔	✔		✔	✔
46. Finding the Peacemakers	ALL	✔	✔			✔	✔
47. Building a "Civilization of Love"	2 - 6	✔	✔	✔	✔	✔	✔
Stage III							
48. Group Brainstorming — Global Issues	2 - 6	✔	✔			✔	
49. "I Messages/You Messages" in Global Issues	2 - 6	✔	✔			✔	
50. We Are All from Different Places	2 - 6	✔					
51. Countries of Origin	2 - 6	✔		✔			
52. Living in Harmony	2 - 6	✔	✔	✔			
53. Oral Reports: Our Countries of Origin	ALL	✔	✔				
54. The Ladder of Peacemaking	ALL	✔	✔	✔		✔	✔
55. We Are Different, We Are the Same	ALL	✔		✔		✔	
56. Being Global Citizens	3 - 6	✔	✔			✔	
57. Murals: A World at Peace	ALL	✔		✔	✔	✔	✔
58. Designing a World Flag	ALL	✔	✔	✔		✔	✔
59. Commitments for the Future	ALL	✔	✔	✔		✔	

CREATING A
PEACEFUL SCHOOL

Remember that as a teacher you have the ability to shape lives.

Let's go on a journey into a domain of education that will enhance all of your teaching and positively impact the lives of your students for years to come. Enjoy the trip, and don't forget to appreciate the process of getting there as much as you enjoy the destination.

THE SKILLS OF PEACEMAKING AND CONFLICT RESOLUTION

The skills include:

- acceptance of self and others
- the ability to communicate with others, including the use of "I Messages"
- acceptance of feelings (one's own and others')
- the willingness to compromise and seek "Win/Win" solutions
- the process of affirming (acknowledging positive qualities in others)

HOW DO I START TEACHING THESE SKILLS?

Start by making yourself the model. In other words, don't just teach the skills, use them yourself in your personal life and with your students. Remember that as a teacher you have the ability to shape lives. The impact you make may last forever with many of your students. By introducing the skills of peacemaking to young children, you are giving your students the opportunity to find new ways to respond to conflict, better ways to communicate, and the potential for healthier relationships. Modeling the behaviors you want to see in your students is the most important thing you can do.

Once you have started using these principles in your own life, you will probably be very pleased with the results. One teacher reported after doing so, "My relationships with my family and friends are improving. I'm communicating with them in more effective ways and it's become a lot easier to work out differences." Remember, though, that this will take some time. At first it may feel awkward and unnatural, but like riding a bike, the more you do it the easier it gets.

WHAT ARE THE SKILLS AND BEHAVIORS I WILL NEED TO MODEL?

The first thing you will need to model is a sense of self-acceptance, a sense that "I'm okay and I accept who I am, my needs, my feelings and my flaws." This, of course, is the same feeling we want to give to each child about himself or herself. We're also modeling the concept, "You're whole and perfect exactly as you are."

The next behavior is one that models, "I am on your side." It's crucial for children to feel accepted by the important adults in their lives. When problems come up it's not necessary to become adversaries, but sometimes we fall into adversarial positions strictly out of habit and from not knowing we have other choices of action. Children need to know we will not betray or abandon them when they've done something wrong. They need to know that we are their partners, and that we are committed to their well-being, no matter what. Beyond all this, children need to know that there are solutions to problems and that together we can find them.

"We can work it out" comes next. An outgrowth of self-acceptance and partnership is the belief that there are solutions to problems. Conflict is a normal and natural part of the process of life. The problem with conflict is the way people choose to work through it. Conflict is not synonymous with aggression. Children need to see this and they need to see that conflict resolution is a dynamic, creative process that can be fun, given the right circumstances.

Children need to see us working out our own conflicts and helping them work out theirs. As teachers we're all aware of how many conflicts come up between ourselves and our students.

A prime example:

Teacher: "Johnny, why didn't you do your homework again?" [angrily]

Johnny: "I don't know." [looks to the floor]

Teacher: "This is the third time this week I've had to speak to you about this. [yelling] You're lazy, Johnny, and I'm going to have to contact your parents."

Johnny: [sad, sullen, and angry] "Go ahead. See if I care!"

Another approach:

Teacher: "Johnny, I'm concerned about the fact that your homework isn't complete. [in a concerned, caring voice] Is there a problem I need to know about?" [hand on Johnny's shoulder]

Johnny: [Looks at teacher and doesn't say anything but makes full eye contact]

Teacher: "If there is some way I can help, I'd like to know. I care about you, Johnny, and I really want to see you do well this year."

Johnny: "I didn't understand the chapter. In fact I have trouble with words in this book every time I try to read it."

Teacher: "Perhaps there is some way we can work on the problem together. Have you talked to your mom and dad about the difficulty you've had with this book?"

Johnny: "No."

Teacher: "Maybe we can all sit down together and find a way to help you." [reassuringly]

In these contrasting examples each teacher cares about the student, but their behavior is motivated by a different attitude. The first teacher's motivation is a sense of her own frustration. She lets this stand in the way of any effective interaction she might have with her student. The second teacher's motivation is a commitment to working it out and having her student feel whole and supported. She accomplishes this, just as you can when you're focused on conciliation as a priority.

Research proves that daily affirmation builds self-esteem.

Affirmation is our final example of modeling. How does one affirm? It's easy. Simply look the recipient in the eyes and give him or her a sincere, positive comment about himself or herself.

Example to a student:

"Jeff, I'm so pleased about the quality of the work you've been doing. It's creative, carefully completed, and always finished on time. Keep up the good work."

To a colleague:

"Mary, I really appreciate all of the great ideas you give me. You're so generous with them. It helps me and my students. Thanks so much. It means a lot."

So often we think positive thoughts about other people but we don't express them. By affirming, we continuously acknowledge the positive things we see in others. What a huge difference we make in their lives when we do this. It's as if the sun comes out each time we affirm. More significantly, research proves that daily affirmation builds self-esteem. Try it and see the wonderful impact.

By now you're probably asking, "What about discipline? This is all very nice but what happens when the kids act up?" We have some suggestions for you in this regard.

DEALING WITH DISCIPLINE

Know your bottom-line standards as a school.

Be sure the children know these standards and that they adhere to them consistently. For example, one bottom-line standard is, "Children don't hurt each other in our school." Students know this, and the minute anyone attempts to deviate from this standard they need to know that their behavior is unacceptable. When necessary, a punishment, such as sitting in a time-out area, missing recess, or having a note sent home to their parents, may be levied.

Be unyielding in the area of standards, and be flexible in almost all other areas.

Children have enormous freedom this way. They know there are certain non-negotiable rules for which they must be 100% responsible always. Beyond this they know there is plenty of choice and freedom. This kind of structure gives them an enormous sense of security and of fairness.

Make the parents your partners.

When you draw up your "Guidelines for a Peaceful Classroom" with your students, copy it for the parents and send it home. Let them know what you're doing with this program. Send home the Win/Win Guidelines for them to post and use at home. Invite them into class to observe conflict resolution lessons. Engage them; they will feel a sense of partnership and know that you are on their side as well as their child's.

USING THE WIN/WIN GUIDELINES

The Win/Win Guidelines for conflict resolution are critical to learning the skills of peacemaking. I present them here as well as in several lessons in this book. The Win/Win Guidelines are the basis for teaching the essential process of conflict resolution.

THE WIN/WIN GUIDELINES

1. Take time for cooling off, if needed. Find alternative ways to express anger.
2. Using "I messages," each person states their feelings and the problem as they see it. No blaming, no name-calling, no interrupting.
3. Each person states the problem as the other person sees it.*
4. Each person states how they are responsible for the problem.*
5. Brainstorm solutions together and choose a solution that satisfies both—a Win/Win solution.
6. Affirm, forgive, or thank.

Optional steps

ABBREVIATED WIN/WIN GUIDELINES

1. Cool off
2. "I message"
3. Say back
4. Take responsibility
5. Brainstorm solutions
6. Affirm, forgive, or thank

When you teach the Win/Win Guidelines, be sure to first go over the following:

RULES FOR USING WIN/WIN GUIDELINES

- Be respectful toward one another.
- Listen while the other person speaks.
- Be honest.
- No blaming, name-calling, or interruptions.
- Work toward a solution both people are comfortable with.

SHOWCASING

Showcasing is especially helpful when teaching conflict resolution. Showcasing simply means that from time to time you work out individual conflicts with the participation of the entire class. The following is a condensed example of a sixth grade teacher's application of showcasing the Win/Win Guidelines during a social studies lesson. In this case, the class is already familiar with the process.

Mandy and Sara are whispering to one another. Suddenly Sara tears up a piece of paper and throws it at Mandy. The teacher stops the lesson.

Teacher: What's going on, girls?

Sara: She wrote something nasty on that paper about me.

Mandy: It wasn't nasty. I was just making a joke.

Sara: Some joke. It wasn't funny, and I think you're a creep.

Other students start whispering and calling out, "What did she say about you, Sara?"

Sara: Just shut up and leave me alone.

Teacher: Enough. Sara, I know you're upset right now, and I'd like to help you and Mandy work this problem out the way we discussed, using the Win/Win Guidelines.

Sara: I don't want to work anything out with her. I hate her.

Teacher: I know you're angry at Mandy, but you're also friends. If you're willing, I can help you work out this difference so you can continue to be friends. Remember, the alternative is that you'll both miss recess tomorrow. Which would you rather do?

Mandy: I guess the Win/Win Guidelines.

Sara: All right. [pouting]

Teacher: Are you able to do it now, or do you need time to cool off? [They both agree to do it now.] I'd like to allow the class to be part of the process so we can all learn how to work out our differences. Is that okay with the two of you?

Mandy: Yes.

Sara: As long as no one makes fun of me.

Teacher: Class, do you agree not to make any put-downs of any kind?

Class: Yes.

Teacher: Good. Let's begin. But I must stress something else first. There's no interrupting. If anyone interrupts, the process stops. [Note: This is vital, or the process can take all day and you will be drained.] Do you all agree? [Everyone

nods.] So we'll start by stating the problem. Let me also remind you that whatever you say has to come from a commitment to resolving the conflict. Okay?

Mandy & Sara: Okay.

Teacher: Would you each describe the problem as you see it? Sara, you go first.

Sara: It's what I said before. She wrote something nasty about me.

Mandy: That's because she said my new shirt is ugly.

Sara: It is ugly.

Teacher: Sara, let me remind you of your commitment to working this out. Otherwise, I won't waste the class time.

Sara: Sorry.

Mandy: I think the problem is that Sara put down what I was wearing. So I put her down to get even.

Teacher: It sounds like you both insulted each other. How did you feel, Mandy, when Sara insulted you?

Mandy: Real angry.

Teacher: How about you, Sara?

Sara: I wanted to hit her.

Teacher: I'm glad you didn't, because problems aren't usually worked out by hitting. Sara, can you pretend you're Mandy just for a moment and state the problem as she sees it?

Sara: Okay. Mandy felt put down by what I said about her shirt. She probably felt embarrassed, too, because I said it in front of the other kids.

Teacher: Thanks, Sara. How about you, Mandy. Can you pretend you're Sara for a moment, and state the problem as she sees it?

Mandy: Okay. Sara got angry because I wrote her a nasty note after she made fun of what I was wearing. Sometimes Sara does that when I ignore her and talk to Melissa.

Teacher: Sara, how are you responsible for the problem?

Sara: I made fun of Mandy's shirt.

Teacher: How are you responsible, Mandy?

Mandy: I wrote her a nasty note.

Teacher: What can the two of you do to avoid having this kind of confrontation again? I'd like you to come up with a lot of different ideas, and the class can make suggestions, too. In the end, you two can decide what would be the best solution.

Sara: She can stop calling me names.

Mandy: Sara can stop making fun of the clothes I wear. I can't help it if she has nicer clothes.

Student: Mandy and Sara can trade clothes sometimes.

Student: Mandy and Sara can go shopping together.

Student: Mandy can include Sara when Melissa's around so she doesn't feel ignored.

Sara: Mandy and I can be more considerate of each other's feelings and stop using put-downs.

Mandy: I can tell Sara when I'm angry with her instead of calling her a name.

Student: You can write each other notes to explain why you're mad at each other instead of using them to insult each other.

Teacher: Sounds like we've got lots of good ideas. Girls, what solution do you want to choose?

Sara: How about if we're more considerate of each other's feelings?

Mandy: Yeah. And we can also just tell each other when we're angry instead of calling names.

Teacher: Thanks, girls. I'm pleased with the way you worked this out. Could you affirm each other?

Sara: Thanks, Mandy and I'm sorry I got so mad.

Mandy: It's okay. I'm sorry too and I'm glad we're still friends.

This process takes about ten minutes and is a valuable group exercise in conflict resolution. Showcasing doesn't need to be done very often, but it's particularly helpful when the class is just beginning to learn the Win/Win Guidelines. The class gets to participate in the process and sees

the outcome. It also serves as a model for future cooperative behavior and problem-solving.

As your students integrate and apply the conflict resolution process, they will need you less and less as mediator. Eventually, they will be able to apply the guidelines without you. They do not have to do every step every time, either. Remember that the ten minutes you take out of your lessons to occasionally showcase conflict resolution skills will pay off over and over again as your students become more cooperative and are able to work out their differences. Once that happens, you can send the "adversaries" off to an area of the room where they can work out their problem.

INTEGRATING WIN/WIN

Here are some tips that will help you and your students integrate Win/Win strategies into your daily interactions. You need not use every step every time. The following steps are sufficient in most conflicts:

- Each person states their feelings and the problem as they see it, using "I Messages." No blaming, no name-calling, no interrupting.

- Brainstorm solutions together and choose a solution that satisfies both parties.

- Affirm your partner.

Reserve the other steps of the guidelines for times you think they would be most useful.

For example, if you find that one or both children are not taking responsibility for their role in the conflict, have them do the step, "Each person states how they are responsible for the problem."

You will soon recognize when you need to implement the various steps. After a while the children will begin to do this on their own, without your help.

Invest time at the beginning of the year.

Taking the time to help your students resolve their conflicts early on really pays off. The students will begin to internalize the principles and strategies of conflict resolution.

Showcasing

"*Showcasing*" conflicts, or mediating in front of the whole class from time to time, allows the other children to observe and participate in the process. It is important to ask permission of the students having the conflict before proceeding.

Use the Clipboard Technique.

Have a clipboard called the "Let's Work It Out" clipboard at your desk. Tell the children they can sign up any time throughout the day if a conflict arises that they need help in mediating. Allow 10-15 minutes at the end of each day, if possible, at which time you can gather your entire class together to review the conflicts and collaboratively brainstorm solutions.

Practice giving "I Messages" ahead of time.

Imagine the following scenario:

The class is noisy. You want them to settle down. You're getting tense. They're not listening. The old way to respond:

"You are too noisy! In fact you are the most unruly group I've ever had. You probably couldn't stop talking if your lives depended on it."

The new way, using "I Messages":

"I'm getting really aggravated because I don't want all this noise. I want you to settle down now. I find it hard to teach when everyone's talking."

Notice that both dialogues express the teacher's feelings. But the first puts down the students, most likely making them feel defensive. The second dialogue is honest, but it focuses more on the teacher's reaction and less on negative labels and sarcasm.

You can have your students practice giving "I Messages" with you and with one another. If you do this fairly often your students will find it easier to give "I Messages" when real conflicts arise, and you will too.

REINFORCEMENT STRATEGIES

It is extremely important for you to use reinforcement strategies. Remember, you'll keep the understandings alive by modeling peacemaking behaviors and by reinforcing the positive. Here are some ways to do so:

1. *Use the "Disciplining With Love"* techniques daily, especially when catching your students in the act of doing what you want. Reinforce their behaviors often.

2. *Do "Peacemaker of the Week" alternate Fridays.* Have the children affirm one another for peacemaking behaviors they have observed in one another throughout the week.

Some schools have their principal involved in this. For example, one principal has lunch with children who have been selected "Peacemaker of the Week" throughout the month. Another principal has monthly assemblies during which the "Peacemakers of the Week" are honored with a certificate. Another principal calls the parents of children who have exhibited peacemaking behaviors, giving them an acknowledgment for the positive things their children have done. What a great experience it is for those parents to hear good news, rather than bad, from the principal.

3. *Logs can also be used to reinforce peacemaking.* Children who are too young to write can draw and/or dictate in their logs.

Some teachers use logs after lessons to allow their students to reflect upon and extend what they have just learned. You can have your children write about the following topics and any other ideas you come up with:

- How you feel when you get angry.

- Choices you make when you're angry at someone.

- Ways you've worked out a conflict with someone in your family or with friends.

- Write about an ongoing conflict you have with someone in your life and ways you can work it out.

- Describe someone you know who acted like a peacemaker. Detail what they did.

- Describe ways you have been a peacemaker recently.

- Focus on someone we have read about (characters in stories, people in the news) and peacemaking behaviors they have exhibited.

4. *Teach the children how to calm themselves with deep breathing.* When the kids get "itchy," stop what you're doing and have them do some deep breathing. Say: "Let's get calm right now by taking a deep breath all the way to the bottom of your abdomen. Expand your stomach as though it's a balloon each time you breathe in. Deflate it each time you breathe out; in through your nose and out through your mouth. Take another breath. Take one more. Now notice how quiet this room has become. Do you feel more relaxed, too?" You can have your children think quiet thoughts as they are breathing deeply. They can recall a time they were resting quietly at home, or a time they sat in a peaceful place outdoors. This technique is invaluable in helping kids calm themselves.

5. *Keep catching your students in the act of "doing it right" instead of "doing it wrong."*

READY, SET, GO

Now you're ready to go. Don't forget to skim through the book before you begin, and please adapt these lessons to your particular classroom or family situation. Dialogue has been included within each lesson to make your job easier, but don't be confined by it. Change the words to fit your style, and bring the richness of your own experiences into each lesson.

As you do each lesson, you might consider sharing personal anecdotes during circle discussions. For example, in Lesson 1 you'll be discussing the idea of a peaceful classroom. Share yours first. It will help the children open up. They'll also appreciate hearing about your feelings and ideas.

Another thing to stress—good listening. As each child speaks, ask every other student in the class to focus on him or her. Ask each child to look directly at the speaker. Begin to have each child ask the rest of the class to look at them when they speak. For example, Shawna is going to share. She looks around the circle and sees other children talking. She says, "Class, could you please look at me, I'd like to share something." Don't let her begin to share until every eye is on her and every ear attuned.

Now, bring the lessons to your students with my best wishes and with deep hope that their futures and yours will be happy, loving, and peaceful.

CREATING A PEER MEDIATION PROGRAM IN YOUR SCHOOL

You can use *Learning the Skills of Peacemaking* as a foundation for setting up a building-wide peer mediation program. In fact, you can train staff and mediators in conflict resolution/peer mediation skills based on selected lessons in this book. In the following chapter, you will learn how to do this, but first let's address the question, "Why peer mediation?"

In recent years hundreds of peer mediation programs have been springing up around the country, for good reason. Research has shown: "Allowing students to be joint architects in matters affecting them promotes feelings of control and autonomy. Students who know how to manage their own conflicts constructively and regulate their own behavior have a developmental advantage over those who do not" (*Educational Leadership*, Sept. 1992).

In its December 1993 issue of "Update," the Association for Supervision and Curriculum Development (ASCD) featured several peer mediation programs, saying, "The most successful programs involve both students and educators... because conflict resolution programs work best where all members of the school community share some common norms and strategies for dealing with conflict. ... Schools should teach all students negotiation and peer mediation skills."

Using conflict resolution in a holistic way, with all staff and students taking part, is the best way to create a peaceful environment in your school. When everyone in the school uses the same skills, the effectiveness increases in volumes.

Peer mediation empowers kids to help one another. When we combine skills for resolving conflicts with a method that allows children to help one another when they are "stuck," we're giving kids the gift of autonomy.

It's not that adults should never be involved in helping kids resolve conflicts—quite the contrary. Adults need to be integrally involved in building the foundation for a peaceful school, including modeling the use of "peacemaking" behaviors, teaching the skills of peacemaking and conflict resolution, reinforcing positive choices, and being available to students when they need extra help in resolving a conflict. However, adults aren't necessarily the best people to approach first when a conflict occurs. It often serves kids better to seek a peer when in need.

Some teachers ask, "When a conflict occurs, do the 'disputants' immediately seek a mediator, or do they try to work out the problem on their own first?" Great question. The following guide provides the answer.

WHEN A CONFLICT OCCURS

FIRST: Children should try to work it out themselves using the Win/Win Guidelines.

SECOND: If the problem does not get resolved, children should seek peer mediators to help them work it out.

THIRD: If a conflict is of a more serious or long-term nature, an appointment should be set up for a formal mediation to be done by peers in the presence of an adult.

FOURTH: If the problem does not get resolved by any of the above, then mediation needs to be done by a skilled adult.

If your entire school community uses peacemaking skills, applies the Win/Win Guidelines during times of conflict, and is committed to having a peaceful school, it will be rare if many conflicts get as far as the fourth step. You'll find that conflict will become more and more self-managing. What a joy that is!

A STEP-BY-STEP GUIDE FOR CREATING A PEER MEDIATION PROGRAM

STEP 1

Each teacher in the building should be teaching the lessons in *Learning the Skills of Peacemaking* at least once a week. This is vital in setting the tone for a peaceful school.

Introduce every staff member to the Win/Win Guidelines so they can use them in conflict situations right away. This includes the principal, all teachers, the school nurse, your child study team, paraprofessionals, classroom volunteers, and anyone else who deals with the children.

Each of these people will serve as a role model for the children. They will also help kids make positive choices when conflicts occur. It is very important that there be uniformity throughout the school: a common language, a common attitude, and a common way of dealing with conflict.

STEP 2

Have teachers introduce every child in your school to the Win/Win Guidelines. Use the lessons in this book to sensitize children to the need for working out differences rather than fighting them out. Peacemaking skills are the primary building block for any effective conflict resolution program.

STEP 3

Form a Conflict Resolution Committee in your school. Invite your principal to take part. If you are fortunate enough to have a student assistance counselor, strongly encourage them to be on the committee. Student assistance counselors are fast becoming our most valuable resource in helping children learn conflict resolution skills.

Your committee will be the backbone of a unified drive to make peacemaking skills an integral part of the school. They will need to meet on a regular basis to do the following:

- plan and conduct trainings
- help select peer mediators
- be available to support staff and students in implementing conflict resolution/peer mediation skills
- help evaluate your school's conflict resolution/peer mediation program
- avail themselves to mediators during appointed mediation sessions

STEP 4

Establish criteria for selection of peer mediator candidates. Here are some questions you can use in doing so:

Is the person under consideration...

- respected by the other students?
- fair and honest?
- using conflict resolution skills in their own life?
- able to honor the confidentiality of others?
- able to be unbiased?
- willing to put in the extra time?
- committed to peacemaking?

In considering all of the above, think in terms of developing a cross-section of mediators, including a balanced number of boys, girls, children of different ethnic backgrounds, and children who have good grades as well as those who are challenged by academics (including special education children).

You may want to consider limiting your candidates to "upper-classmen." For example, a K-6 school might select mediators from the fourth, fifth, and sixth grades only. That's what many schools do. However, some researchers suggest that we train every child in every class to be peer mediators, rotating mediation duties among members of each class (David W. Johnson and Roger T. Johnson, *Teaching Students to Be Peacemakers*). There are many different ways to run a program. Decide which one will serve your school best.

Some schools consider their "negative role models," children who might be turned around by participating in a peer mediation program, as possible candidates. If a child is exhibiting many of the aforementioned criteria, but is channeling their energy into negative behaviors, you may want to think about involving them in your school's program. Sometimes this serves the child as well as the school.

Be careful not to set up an elite group of children the others can't identify with. Peer mediators should be a representative sample of your student body. As one of our mediators said, "I don't want the kids to think I'm some dork walking around with a button and telling other people what to do."

STEP 5

Ask for nominations from the student body. You can use the form on page 28. Members of the Conflict Resolution Committee can visit each class, passing out nomination forms and explaining the criteria for selection. If you choose, you can have each classroom teacher do this with their own students. Make sure the children are nominating candidates based on the criteria, not on popularity. Children can also nominate themselves. You'd be surprised how astute kids can be in self-selecting and in selecting one another.

STEP 6

Application forms now need to be given out to all children nominated for the position of peer mediator. See page 29 for a form you can use or adapt.

STEP 7

The actual screening process now begins. The committee needs to go over all applications. You may want to interview some of the children, especially those who might not be known by someone on the committee. Seek the input of the candidate's teachers if you need more information.

When making your selections, remember to create a cross-section of students. Select more mediator candidates than you plan to end up with because some may end up dropping out.

You should try to end up with at least one mediator for every fifteen students.

STEP 8

Now is a good time to decide when and where mediations are going to take place.

Some schools find it most useful to have specific areas of the building designated for mediations. For example, you can have a table in your cafeteria set up as a "mediation table" where two mediators are always available to help children resolve lunch-time conflicts.

A spot on the playground can also be designated for use during recess. Two mediators should always be available in that area.

In some schools, the office is the place where kids go to have conflicts mediated at other times throughout the day. A student assistance counselor's space, if available, is another good spot. Members of the Conflict Resolution Committee can schedule mediation time in their rooms during free periods if they choose.

One other thing. You'll need to have your mediators designated by something easily identifiable. Some schools have their mediators wear special hats or T-shirts. We have found buttons to be a better option because they're easy to spot but less obtrusive. In trying to avoid the mediators coming across as some kind of elite force, we wanted to have them wear something that spoke, not shouted, to the other kids. Buttons seemed to work well.

STEP 9

The training phase now begins. Your staff needs to be trained first so that they fully understand how to support a peer mediation program in your building. Their role in teaching, reinforcing and encouraging their students to use conflict resolution skills is vital. This training should take about an hour and can be done after school.

Be sure to include the following:

- Review the Win/Win Guidelines and the Rules for Using Win/Win, making sure that everyone fully understands how to use and apply them.

- Go over the role of your peer mediators, and ask your staff for their support of the program.

Remind them that this is something new for all of you and that you will need their help in smoothing out the kinks.

Remind them that the job of the mediators is not to solve problems for other kids. It's simply to help others when they get stuck.

- Go over such logistics as where mediations will take place, when, and how to handle the issue of releasing children from class. Your committee will need to address all of these questions prior to the training.

- Show whatever you are going to use to designate your mediators (button, cap, T-shirt). Remind the staff of their important role in encouraging students to seek out mediators when there's difficulty working out a conflict.

- Pass out copies of the Win/Win Guidelines and Rules for Win/Win, to be posted in every room of the building.

- Leave plenty of time for questions and discussion. Remind people that the entire school will benefit by your working together.

STEP 10

Now it's time to train your mediators. The Conflict Resolution Committee can decide among themselves who will lead this training. If you have a student assistance counselor, they would be the ideal person to co-lead the training with another committee member. It will take a total of about five hours to train your mediators. It's most effective to break this up into two ninety-minute blocks of time and a third session lasting two hours, leaving time in between each session for students to digest what they have learned.

Now refer to pages 33 and 34 for your "Peer Mediator Training Guide." This will give you a step-by-step outline of everything you will need to do to train your mediators.

STEP 11

Congratulations! You have completed your training sessions. You are now ready to introduce your peer mediators to the student body. A great way to do this is to hold a special assembly to kick off the program.

During the assembly you can explain the purpose of the peer mediation program, letting everyone know that the mediators are available to help them work out their conflicts when they get "stuck." Reiterate the value of having a peaceful school and each person's importance in making this happen. Tell the kids they'll be able to seek out mediators when needed, and to let their teachers know if they wish to set up an appointment for a mediation.

Your principal or a Conflict Resolution Committee member may want to co-lead this assembly, using the time to "psych up" the students about peacemaking and do some community-building. Here are some things you can do to build a sense of spirit and harmony:

- Have a group of students create and present a skit about resolving conflicts. They can play act a before-and-after situation, showing how a conflict might have been handled before the students knew how to do so peacefully, and then how the outcome changes after they are taught to use conflict resolution skills.

- Prior to the assembly, videotape children play acting a conflict situation. Show the conflict being resolved with the help of mediators. Show the videotape during the assembly.

- Select a unifying song like "We Are Family" that the student body can sing together. Have them sing it each time they are all together.

- Display projects the children have made based on the lessons in this book. "A Peaceful School Looks Like This" is a good one to use. It would be great to have murals from every class in the school.

- Announce a "Peacemaker of the Month" program where school-wide peacemakers will be honored. You can hold a monthly assembly for this purpose, or the names can be announced over the loudspeaker. You can also have a special bulletin board designated for your peacemakers of the month.

One school honors their peacemakers of the month with "Lunch with the Principal." Come up with your own ideas. The more you can do to build community and create enthusiasm for peacemaking, the better, and the kids will love it.

STEP 12

Have regularly scheduled meetings with your mediators to get feedback from them about how their mediations have been going. Use the time to air questions, problem-solve, play act for extra practice, and enable the mediators to learn from one another's experiences.

Make sure your mediators have been using their notebooks to indicate each time they have completed a mediation. Have them refer to notes they have on mediations they've taken part in. Discuss these at your meetings. Keep records of how many mediations are being completed each month. This is important data for you to have in evaluating your program.

STEP 13

Evaluate your program at the end of the year. You will find program evaluation forms for this purpose beginning on page 30. Be sure to include how many mediations have taken place throughout the year.

During your final Conflict Resolution Committee meeting you'll want to review your evaluation forms and make decisions about changes for the following year.

Good luck in creating your school as a community that lives peacemaking in every way. Picture each person as a link in a chain: the principal, teachers, support staff, parents, and the children. Imagine each link supporting the other, bringing together threads of peace, harmony, and respect. The more we spread peacemaking to those around us, the stronger the chain that bonds each link together. May your school be its living image.

PEER MEDIATOR STUDENT NOMINATION FORM

I would like to nominate the following student as a peer mediator candidate:

_____

(Student's name)

Here's why I think this person would be a good peer mediator:

_____   _____

Signature   Date

PEER MEDIATOR APPLICATION FORM

Name _____

Date _____

I would like to be considered for the position of peer mediator. Here are the reasons I think I would do a good job:

List any other qualities you have or personal experiences you have had that would make you a good peer mediator:

I understand that if chosen to be a peer mediator I will respect the confidentiality of anyone I work with.

_____
Signature

PEER MEDIATION EVALUATION FORM
(for mediators)

Name _____

Date _____

How many mediations have you taken part in? _____

How many were concluded successfully? _____

Do you feel you were able to help the majority of the people you worked with? Explain.

How do you think your peers feel about our peer mediation program? Explain.

How was being a mediator a positive experience?

What have you learned by being a mediator?

Were there any negative aspects of your experience? Explain.

How can we improve the program? (use the back if necessary)

PEER MEDIATION EVALUATION FORM
(for staff)

Name _____

Date _____

Do you feel the peer mediation program has helped our school? How?

What changes have you seen in our school since the peer mediation program?

How do you think we can improve the program?

PEER MEDIATION EVALUATION FORM
(for students)

Name _____

Date _____

Have you used the services of a peer mediator this year? Why or why not?

Did you find these services helpful? Why or why not?

What kinds of changes have you seen in our school since this program?

Do you feel the majority of kids use peer mediation? Why or why not?

How do you feel we can improve the program?

PEER MEDIATION TRAINING GUIDE

CONTENT TO BE INCLUDED IN YOUR TRAINING SESSIONS

You'll be able to base much of the content in your trainings on information in the following lessons of this book, so be sure to review these lessons carefully ahead of time:

Lesson 9   Using "I Messages"

Lesson 10   Win/Win Guidelines

Lesson 12   Reflective Listening

Lesson 15   Brainstorming Solutions to Conflicts

In addition, be sure to carefully review pages 17-21. Much of your content for the training workshop is covered in these pages.

"Cooperative Group Mediation" (this page) is another essential part of mediator training. Review it carefully. You will be able to cover the content necessary for mediator training in approximately five hours. You will find a suggested schedule on pages 39-40.

CLARIFYING THE ROLE OF THE MEDIATOR

The role of peer mediators is to help children resolve their own conflicts using the Win/Win Guidelines. Train your mediators to work in pairs. Kids usually find it more comfortable to work with a partner, either taking turns facilitating each step of the Win/Win Guidelines or having one person lead and the other jump in if the process gets off-track. In this case mediators will alternate taking the lead position with each new mediation.

During the training, always stress that mediators don't solve other people's problems. Instead, they engage disputants in the process of talking to each other face to face to work out their own solutions.

Keep reinforcing this as you train, because you'll find that the natural inclination is to give advice. We all do it. If someone comes to us with a problem, we usually want to solve it for them. If we come up with the solution, the people with the problem have gained far less than they would have by coming up with their own. When people solve problems they're faced with, they are empowered. That's the purpose of this program: to empower each child to find acceptable solutions to problems that arise in their relationships.

Here's another important distinction for mediators to reinforce in all conflict situations:

WHEN IN CONFLICT, REMEMBER, IT'S US AGAINST THE PROBLEM, NOT US AGAINST EACH OTHER.

(from *Mediation for Kids*, Schmidt et al.)

When we remember this, it shifts the attitude from adversarial to conciliatory. In the old mode of thinking about conflict, we saw ourselves as pitted against each other and working to save face or defend turf. As we shift, we begin to see that many of our past problems have arisen from seeing the other person as the enemy.

Peacemaking helps us see that the concept of enemy exists primarily in our minds. We fare better by attacking the problem, not the other person. Keep reinforcing this concept throughout your mediator training sessions. Make sure it is reinforced during your staff training as well.

COOPERATIVE GROUP MEDIATION

The most valuable part of mediation training is play acting conflicts and practicing mediating them. On the following page, you will find a technique that can be used not only for mediation training, but also in teaching classes how to resolve conflicts. Use this technique in training staff and parents as well. It is highly effective and fun to do.

At the end of this section, you will find conflict scenarios that you can use for simulations.

During your training sessions, put them on a transparency and project them for the whole group to see. See Appendix, pages 236-240.

COOPERATIVE GROUP MEDIATION: A STEP-BY-STEP APPROACH

1. Arrange circles with five students in each cooperative group. Using the simulations on pages 37 and 38, everyone in the group will have one of the following roles. These roles will rotate with each succeeding simulation:

- Mediator 1
- Mediator 2
- Disputant A
- Disputant B
- Observer/recorder

2. Explain the roles:

Mediators work together to help disputants resolve their conflict. They can take turns, each facilitating succeeding steps of the Win/Win Guidelines, or they can choose one to be lead mediator with the other helping out as moral support and giving input if the process gets stuck.

Disputants play this role from the vantage point of people who have been trained in conflict resolution. Remember, the first step in making your peer mediation program work is to teach every student how to use the Win/Win Guidelines. When doing simulations, disputants must keep in mind that they are play acting people who are familiar with the process, treating each other respectfully.

Observer/recorder takes notes as the simulation proceeds. Their job is to give feedback to mediators and disputants. At the end of this section you will find an Observation Record Sheet for the observer/recorder to fill out during the mediation.

3. Project one at a time the simulations listed on pages 37 and 38, on a screen large enough for all participants to see.

4. Have the students in each group decide among themselves who will play each part for the first simulation, reminding them that roles will rotate.

5. Let the participants know that the workshop leaders will be circulating among them, taking notes as they play act, and that feedback will be given at the end of each simulation.

6. Have the disputants position their chairs so they can look at each other directly.

7. Using the Mediation Script on the following page, mediators begin the mediation process.

8. Workshop leaders circulate, taking notes. You can also use the Observation Record Sheet on page 36. If any of the people playing the part of mediators run into problems, help them out. For example, you might say, "Try paraphrasing what you just heard Susie say." Or, "Tommy and Jason have had enough time to discuss what they're upset about. Have them go on to the next step."

Don't take over. Just interject whatever comment is needed to move the process along. Then go on to the next group and do the same.

9. After about ten minutes, let the groups know that they should start wrapping up the simulation and hearing from their observer/recorder. Have them do their group debriefing for about five minutes.

10. Have the groups direct their attention to the Workshop Leaders. Give feedback to each group, and at the same time ask the group's observer/recorder to share comments and insights with all participants. This process enables the students to learn from one another's experiences in the simulation activity. Other members of each group can share as well.

This part of the process should take ten to fifteen minutes.

11. Go on to the next simulation. Repeat the process.

MEDIATION SCRIPT

1. "Have you both cooled off? If not, what can you do to calm down before we start talking about this?"

Mediators can encourage disputants to take a deep breath, get a drink of water, or go to different places and sit down for a little while in order to cool off. If either disputant is still showing strong signs of anger, schedule the mediation for a later time, or even for the next day.

When they are sufficiently cooled off, go to step 2.

2. "I'd like to remind you of our Rules for Win/Win."
State them:

• Be respectful toward one another.

• Listen while the other person speaks.

• Be honest.

• No blaming, name-calling, or interrupting.

• Work toward a solution that both people are comfortable with.

"Are you each willing to abide by these rules?" (Make sure they are.)

3. "Please look at each other. Person A, would you give person B an 'I Message' and explain what's on your mind."

4. "Person B, would you give Person A an 'I Message' and explain what's on your mind."

5. Mediator paraphrases what both parties have said.

6. "A, would you tell B what you heard him say he is upset about. It would be helpful to start with the words, 'I heard you say. ...' "

7. "B, would you tell A what he said he is upset about."

8. Let them discuss the problem, but don't let it turn into a bicker session.

9. "A, how were you responsible for this problem?"

10. "B, how were you responsible for this problem?"

11. Mediator reflects back what has been said.

12. "What can you do to solve this problem?" Have them talk about it, encouraging them to come up with several solutions. Have them choose one or two together.

13. "Are you both comfortable with the solution?" Acknowledge them both for working out their problem.

14. Have the students affirm, thank, or forgive each other. A handshake can be given now. Mediators should thank children for the good job they did.

NOTE: In some cases it will help the children if their solutions or agreements are written down. This can be done at the end of the mediation process.

Don't forget to have mediators mark a tally in their pocket-sized notebooks each time a mediation is completed. Mediators should also indicate whether or not the mediation was successfully completed. They can jot down notes on anything they might want to discuss at their next meeting.

OBSERVATION RECORD SHEET
(for use during simulations)

1. Have the mediators made sure the disputants are sufficiently cooled off?

2. Are the mediators keeping the disputants on track?

3. Are the mediators reflecting back from time to time what has been said?

4. Are the disputants treating each other with respect?

5. Are the disputants working toward a solution?

6. Did the disputants reach a solution? If so, how did the mediators help this happen?

7. Is there anything the mediators might want to do differently next time?

COOPERATIVE GROUP SIMULATIONS

Simulation #1

Second graders Amy and Susie are good friends. They play together on the playground every day. Today Amy decides to play with Jessica instead. When Susie asks to join in they each say "No." When the class goes inside Susie knocks Amy's books off her desk. Amy responds by doing the same to Jessica.

Amy's point of view: I like to play with Susie but Jessica's been asking me to play with her for a while now. Jessica and I had just decided to go on the seesaw together when Susie came over. There's not room for three people on the seesaw so we told Susie she couldn't play with us. We didn't mean to hurt her feelings.

Susie's point of view: Amy and I play together every day. She never told me she wanted to play with anyone else. I can't believe that she and Jessica just left me out when I asked them to play. I would never do that to Amy.

Simulation #2

Fifth graders Jamal and Peter are very competitive with one another. Every day they each rush to be first in line. Today Jamal gets in line first. He moves out of his place for a moment to pick up a paper that fell down. Peter rushes into first place in line. When Jamal sees this, he pushes Peter out of line. Peter calls him a name.

Peter's point of view: Every day Jamal tries to be first. Sometimes he "cuts" me in line. Today he got out of his place, so I should be able to be first, right? He had no right to push me.

Jamal's point of view: Every day Peter tries to be first in line. Sometimes he "cuts" me to get there. Before, I just bent over for a second to pick up a paper, and Peter comes rushing up and gets in my spot. It's not fair for someone to do that. He had no right.

Simulation #3

Fourth graders Luz and Stephanie never liked each other. Every time Luz walks by, Stephanie gives her a look or whispers negative things under her breath. Today Luz has had enough. When Stephanie makes a face at her, Luz grabs Stephanie's hair and pulls it hard.

Stephanie's point of view: I hate Luz. She's always been mean to me. When we were in first grade, she stole my best friend away from me, and I've never forgiven her for it. She always walks right by me and ignores me. I don't think I'm doing anything so bad.

Luz's point of view: Stephanie hates me and I don't know why. She always gives me looks and whispers behind my back. My mother told me to just ignore her, which I try to do, but she keeps on being mean to me. Today I couldn't take it anymore so I pulled her hair. I know it wasn't right, but how much can a person take?

Simulation #4

Fifth grader Lewis has a crush on his classmate, Marcy. Marcy wants nothing to do with him. Lewis always sends Marcy notes and says things that make her feel embarrassed. Marcy usually responds by walking away. Today Lewis sneaks up behind Marcy, puts his arm around her shoulder, and calls her "Sweet thing." Marcy responds by pushing him away and saying, "Get out of here, nerd." Lewis responds by using a swear word.

Marcy's point of view: Lewis won't leave me alone. I don't want to hang out with him. I've made that clear, but he still keeps bothering me, sending me these creepy notes and sometimes even touching me. I called him a nerd just to get him off me, once and for all.

Lewis' point of view: Marcy is the prettiest girl in the class. I want to be with her. I figured she's playing hard to get and if she knows how much I like her, maybe she'd cut me a break. Before, she really shot me down in front of my friends. No girl gets away with that.

Simulation #5

Roger's father beat him up him this morning. This happens often. Roger is in a foul mood when he arrives on the school bus. In walks smiling happy Jeremy, who's always in a good mood. Roger hates Jeremy for his good moods, thinking that Jeremy's life is probably a lot better than his own. He sticks his foot out as Jeremy walks down the aisle of the bus, tripping him hard. Jeremy looks up in shock and punches Roger.

Roger's point of view: My father beats me up all the time. I can't stand living in my house. Jeremy must think he's better than me. He always has nice clothes, and his father even coaches the basketball team. I can't stand seeing that confident smile on his face each day so I tripped him. I wanted to knock him down a few pegs.

Jeremy's point of view: I'm getting on the bus this morning, not bothering anyone, and all of a sudden that kid Roger sticks his foot out and trips me. I hardly even know the kid. Why would he want to hurt me? I hit my head real hard on the edge of the seat. I was so mad I punched him.

NOTE: Refer to the Appendix at the end of this book for each example of play acting on a separate page, suitable for reproducing on a transparency.

SCHEDULE AND CONTENT FOR PEER MEDIATOR TRAINING SESSIONS

DAY ONE: 90 MINUTES

1. **Welcome and congratulate mediators.** Have them introduce themselves.

2. **Go over purpose of peer mediators.** Tell participants what will be covered today.

3. **Warm up activity:**

Have children face each other in pairs. Have them choose a Person A and a Person B.

Person A asks Person B, "What's something you're really good at? Describe it for me." Now B asks A the same question.

Next have the children form a large circle. Each partner tells the group what the other partner has said.

4. **Review the Win/Win Guidelines,** demonstrating each step. Go over the Abbreviated Win/Win also. In simple conflicts, it's easier to use the abbreviated version (page 17).

5. **Go over the Rules for Using Win/Win Guidelines** (page 17). Let mediators know that each time they do a mediation they'll need to remind the disputants of these rules.

6. **Go over "I Messages."** Have the children change "You Messages" into "I Messages." Use Lesson 9 (page 73) and add more "You Messages" of your own.

7. **Practice "Reflective Listening."** Use Lesson 12 (page 85). You can also play the following game called, "Why Are You Mad at Me?":

Have the entire group form a circle. The Workshop Leader asks the first child: "Why are you mad at me?" The first child gets to make up an answer. The Workshop Leader simply paraphrases what has been said. Don't give any other explanation or response, simply reflect back what is said.

The first child now turns to the second child and asks the same question. The question goes around the circle with each person paraphrasing what they have heard.

After each person has had a chance to listen and paraphrase, talk about what it felt like to do exactly that: to just plain listen without offering a response, defense, or explanation.

Let the kids know that this is a vital skill in conflict resolution. Tell them that they will be practicing it for homework.

8. **Assign homework.** Pass out Peer Mediation Logs. You can use a simple composition notebook for this purpose. During the following week have the children do the following:

   a. Use "I Messages" any time you need to express your feelings to another person.

   b. Use the technique of Reflective Listening as often as you can, even in day-to-day conversations with people.

   c. If you have a conflict with anyone, use the Win/Win Guidelines to work it out.

   d. Every night write in your log about how it felt to do the above and what kind of responses you got. Bring your log to the next training session and be prepared to share.

NOTE: Refreshments are a good idea at all of your sessions.

DAY TWO: 90 MINUTES

1. **Welcome everyone back.** Congratulate them on completing their first week of Peer Mediation Training.

2. **Paired share:** Children share with a partner what it was like using "I Messages" and doing "Reflective Listening" throughout the week. Have them talk about any opportunities they've had to use the Win/Win Guidelines throughout the week. Children can read from their logs if they choose.

Now have participants form a large circle and share what they discussed with their partners, bringing to light any new insights they have discovered.

3. **Cooperative Group Simulations:** Leaders demonstrate mediating a conflict. If you have made a video showing a mediation, share that too.

Now refer to the sections on Cooperative Group Mediation (page 34) and Cooperative Group Simulations (page 37) and begin the process. You should probably be able to cover two simulations in the time you have. Be sure to leave plenty of time for debriefing between simulations.

4. **Assign Homework:** Have the children continue to use "I Messages," "Reflective Listening," and Win/Win throughout the week.

Have them continue to write their responses, using these processes. This time have them include in their logs how they feel about the prospect of becoming peer mediators. They can jot down what else they would like to practice to do the job well.

Have them bring their weekly schedules next time.

DAY THREE: 2 HOURS

1. **Welcome** the children and let them know that by the end of this session they will be official peer mediators.

2. **Go over logs** and any insights the children have gained during the week.

3. **Review the role of peer mediators** again, stressing the necessity to be non-judgmental and to promote respectful interactions. Bring up the issue of confidentiality, making sure that everyone is perfectly clear on what that entails.

> **Stress the need for mediators to use their expertise in allowing other people to solve their own problems rather than doing it for them.**

4. **Cooperative Group Role Simulations:** Do three today. This will be the last practice session before the children actually begin. If you feel they need more practice, you can do so at your next scheduled meeting.

5. **Questions, discussion.**

6. **Set up a schedule** for mediations. Be sure to post it in a place your mediators can refer to.

7. **Award mediators buttons and certificates.** Give them each their pocket notebook and explain how it is to be used. Congratulate them all.

Celebrate!

DEVELOPING AND LEADING PARENT WORKSHOPS

Over the ten years I have been leading workshops, I have found parents to be among the most eager of audiences. Parents are hungry for information on peacemaking skills. They acknowledge that in today's changing world they need new ways to communicate with their families, help children express feelings, and mediate conflicts. One of their prime concerns is how to build peace in the family.

Having children of my own, I echo this concern and can personally attest to the difference peacemaking skills have made in my own family. The impact of my children's growing up in a "peaceful family" makes itself known day after day.

A recent example comes from my son Mike, now a sophomore in college. During one of our weekly phone calls I allowed my questions to become a little too personal, thereby stepping over the line from concerned parent to meddlesome mom. I realized I had gotten Mike quite aggravated with my prying (I can't help myself sometimes!)

Rather than throwing his wrath at me, Mike delivered the perfect "I Message," saying, "Mom, I know you like to show your loving concern for me, but I'm not comfortable when you ask all these questions. I want you to respect my privacy more." Beyond my embarrassment for intruding on my son's boundaries was a sense of pride that he had learned the lessons of peacemaking so well.

I mention this anecdote because it exemplifies something we all strive for—the experience of seeing our children growing up applying valuable lessons learned at home.

Each time I lead workshops for parents I hope that the knowledge and insight they gain will manifest in a higher degree of harmony for their families, the essence of which will be carried by their children into adulthood.

Use this next section to lead parent workshops. Adapt it to suit your particular needs, and have fun bringing the skills of peacemaking beyond the walls of the classroom and into the hearts of families in your community. They will be most grateful.

A STEP-BY-STEP GUIDE TO LEADING PARENT WORKSHOPS

1. **SELECT WORKSHOP LEADERS.** Who are the strongest teachers of peacemaking in your school? Ask them to lead or co-lead this workshop. Let them know that the skills of peacemaking have no age boundaries. The more parents can use these skills at home with their children, the more everyone profits. Having this workshop solidifies the home-school peacemaking connection.

2. **PICK A TIME TO HAVE THE WORKSHOP.** Your workshop should be scheduled at a time convenient for both parents to attend. If possible, try to provide on-site babysitting.

Some of the best workshops I have facilitated featured short demonstrations of lessons from this book involving children. You may want to consider making this a part of your workshop. Parents love seeing the program in action. It also helps them understand the skills they will apply at home. If you choose to involve children in this way, be sure the time you pick is convenient for them.

If you're going to have babysitting, your younger "demonstration children" can be taken care of during the times they are not involved in the workshop.

3. **GO OVER CONTENT FOR THE WORK-SHOP.** Much of the information you'll need will come directly from this book. "Using This Guide: Notes For Teachers and Parents," particularly "Disciplining With Love: Some Guidelines" (pp. 7-9) will form the foundation of your workshop. Each heading in "Disciplining With Love" can be listed on a transparency or chart.

You'll also need a chart and transparencies showing the Win/Win Guidelines, full and abbreviated (pp. 77-78) and Rules for Using Win/Win (page 79). Study the chapter entitled, "Creating a Peaceful Classroom" (pp. 49-50). This will be another major part of your workshop. It's a good idea to have the full and abbreviated Win/Win Guidelines hanging up in the room for the parents to refer to at all times. When it's time to teach each step, you can refer to your transparency.

Refer to "Cooperative Group Mediation" on page 34. Go over this section very carefully. This process will allow parents to mediate conflicts using the Win/Win Guidelines. Be sure to put the simulations on a transparency too (Appendix).

Make copies of "Disciplining With Love," the Win/Win Guidelines, and the abbreviated Win/Win Guidelines, to be distributed on the night of the workshop.

4. **CONSIDER MAKING A VIDEOTAPE.** Many wonderful moments with children can be captured on videotape during peacemaking lessons. This can be another valuable part of your workshop. A simulation using the Win/Win Guidelines or an excerpt from a variety of other lessons often lends itself beautifully to this purpose. A demonstration of "Affirming" is another good one. A ten-minute video can say more about peacemaking than even the best retelling of a classroom experience.

5. **INVOLVE YOUR P.T.A.** Having the support of your building's parent group is a real asset. Often the P.T.A. will publicize the workshop, help prepare for it, and provide refreshments. Making the parents a part of the planning is in keeping with one of the main purposes of the workshop: nurturing the home-school connection.

6. **SAVE WORK FROM THE CHILDREN.** There are many projects in this book that children can make. Often teachers have wonderful murals or art projects from related peacemaking lessons hanging in their rooms. Display such visuals during the workshop. They will brighten up the room and will be another demonstration of what peacemaking is about.

7. **PLAN TO PROVIDE NAMETAGS.** If you have each participant write their first name large enough for workshop leaders to see, you'll provide the key to a much more personal workshop. When people are addressed by name, the comfort level goes way up, and the degree and quality of sharing are increased.

8. **SEND HOME INTERESTING WORK-SHOP ANNOUNCEMENTS.** Be sure to mention how this workshop ties in to the peacemaking program being done in school. If you're going to provide babysitting, mention this prominently. Send your announcements home in plenty of time for people to make the necessary arrangements.

SUGGESTED WORKSHOP SCHEDULE (TWO-HOUR TIME PERIOD)

Welcome the parents. Introduce the program and workshop leaders. Tell the parents what you plan to cover and how it relates to the peacemaking program being done with the children in your school. (5 min.)

Do a warm-up activity. Involve the parents right away by asking, "What do you most want to get out of tonight's workshop?" If you have under 25 participants, you can have each person share their response with the entire group. If your group is too large to accomplish this within ten minutes, have each participant share with the person they are sitting next to (paired sharing). Be sure to have each person introduce themselves before speaking. (10 min.)

Introduce "Disciplining With Love." Use your transparency to go over each step. Be sure to give personal examples. If you have decided to do a video, this might be a good time to show it. For example, a video excerpt from the lesson on affirming would beautifully exemplify step two of the guidelines for disciplining with love. (15 min.)

Introduce the Win/Win Guidelines. Go over each step. If you have children participating in a demonstration lesson, you might want to have them do some simulations showing the use of the guidelines. Otherwise, workshop leaders and other teachers can demonstrate.

Here are some activities to involve the parents for each guideline. This section should take about 30 minutes.

Cooling Off: Have the parents brainstorm ways to cool off. List their responses on a chart. Remind parents that people can't resolve conflicts when they're emotionally upset or angry and that cooling off is an essential first step in conflict resolution.

Let the parents know that it's acceptable to wait, even until the next day, before trying to resolve a conflict, if that's what's needed for both parties to be sufficiently cooled off. The important thing is that both parties get together at some point to resolve the problem.

"I Messages": Give examples of "I Messages" in contrast to "You Messages" and play act the delivery of each. Refer to Lesson 9, "Using 'I Messages' (page 73)." Have the participants change some of the "You Messages" listed in this chapter to "I Messages."

Reflective Listening: Workshop leaders can do some simulations of ways they paraphrase what they hear each other saying.

EXAMPLE:

A. I'm really aggravated that you were late picking me up tonight.

B. I heard you say you're upset about the fact that I was late coming to get you tonight.

(You can prepare some more of these simple simulations ahead of time.)

Next have participants play the reflective listening game, "Why Are You Mad at Me?" (page 39, #7).

This is an excellent technique for allowing people to experience what it's like to just plain listen without giving an opinion or explanation. They also get to experience what it feels like to be truly heard when they speak (an unusual occurrence for many).

Taking Responsibility: No exercise here, just some reminders. Tell participants that in 99 percent of all conflicts, both people are responsible in some way. It's essential that each person be willing to do a little self-examination and take ownership of their role in the problem.

This is a major shift in attitude for most people. It signifies our moving away from an adversarial mode into one of conciliation. When we take responsibility for our role in a conflict, we demonstrate our willingness to work it out. Blame escalates problems; acknowledgment of responsibility helps to solve them.

Brainstorm Solutions: Pose a typical conflict in the home, like two children fighting over which program to watch on TV. Have participants brainstorm as many solutions to this problem as possible, and put them on a large chart. The more the better. This allows parents to see that there are usually many solutions within our reach.

As people become aware of the array of solutions available, a light goes on. They realize that they often have relied on old automatic responses to problems. They start broadening their thinking, seeing that the old way of dealing with conflict is self-limiting. Over time, the quest for new solutions becomes more and more natural.

Affirm, Forgive, Thank: Now is a good time to have the parents do an affirmation exercise in pairs. See Lesson 6 (page 65), "The Process of Affirming." Workshop leaders should demonstrate first.

Cooperative Group Simulations. Now it's time to have your participants practice helping resolve a conflict using the Win/Win Guidelines. The technique is thoroughly described on pages 33 and 34 of this book. Plan to do two simulations, if possible, with some debriefing in between. (25 min.)

Closing: Take any remaining questions. (If you're like me, you'll be overtime by now. Do the best you can, and apologize if you run over. People are usually so grateful for the information you've given them, they're not even aware of the time.) If you're serving refreshments at the end of the evening, you can take more questions then.

Good Luck!

NOTE: Some schools have formed after-school parent/child peacemaking groups as a follow-up to this workshop. The purpose is to practice peacemaking skills (affirming, using the Win/Win Guidelines, practicing reflective listening, etc.) and to work on resolving actual conflicts that have come up at home.

Groups usually meet once a week for six weeks, at which time people have the option of continuing. These groups are extremely helpful to families. If you can set one up in your school, you'll be very pleased with the results.

STAGE I:
PEACE BEGINS WITH ME

"...I speak of a futuristic ideal which exalts wisdom, sensitivity, fairness, and compassion as basic requirements in running the affairs of the world. A new world, the world I long for, cannot be built with the tools, psychology, or belief system of old. It will be born of the changes encoded in the details of our lives as we are living them now. The fabric of the new society will be made of nothing more or less than the threads woven in today's interactions."

Pam McAllister,
Reweaving the Web of Life

CREATING A PEACEFUL CLASSROOM

OBJECTIVES

- The teacher and students will create the setting for a peaceful classroom.
- The students will list qualities of a peaceful classroom.

MATERIALS

- Two large pieces of chart paper
- Markers
- Copies of the Parent letter (see page 51)
- "Friends" (see page 52)

PROCEDURE

1. Think of every child in your class as whole, perfect, and capable. Focus on the promise of each child and imagine this year being the realization of this promise. Also, think about the promise of you, as teacher, impacting your students for the rest of their lives out of the way you interact with them this year. Think of your students as responsible, productive, and caring individuals. Know that you have the ability to help them develop in this way. Now you are ready to have a dialogue with your students.

2. Ask students to sit in a circle either on the floor or in chairs. The circle connects them visually and allows them to see one another. It is helpful to have a permanent space in the room where you can easily form a circle.

3. Say, "Out of my care for you, I want to find new ways to have a peaceful future. We often hear about people hurting each other or not caring about one another. I started to picture what the world would be like if teachers everywhere began to teach their students how to get along and accept other people. What kind of world would it be? Peace starts with each individual, and the way you act affects the world around you." Allow the children to respond.

4. Express your interest in getting to know each student and your willingness to be there for them if they have a problem. You might say something like, "I want us to have a great year together. Out of our cooperation and care for one another we can all help to make this happen."

5. Speak about the need for everyone in the class to work as partners, to cooperate, and to be considerate. Discuss the meaning of the word "considerate." Stress the need for each member to take responsibility for having a peaceful atmosphere in the class. Ask, "What does taking responsibility mean to you?" Discuss.

6. Ask, "How do you want it to be in our room throughout the year? How do you want to be treated and how do you want to treat others?" You can begin by stating some of the ways you would like the class to be. (Example: I want the children to be considerate of one another.)

7. After the children have discussed the kind of class atmosphere they want, you can label this atmosphere as "peaceful." On a piece of chart paper write: A Peaceful Classroom Is One in Which…

8. Ask your students to reiterate the qualities of a peaceful classroom on the chart. It may start something like this: "A peaceful classroom is one in which… we are considerate of each other. We speak quietly. We pay attention when someone else is speaking. We don't call each other names." You can keep expanding this chart throughout the year.

9. After you complete the chart together, ask the children what a "non-peaceful" classroom might be like. Discuss. Ask what it would take, on the part of each student, to have the class be the way they want it to be. Discuss.

10. Ask your students if they will all agree to do whatever it takes to create a peaceful classroom

and bring to life what they listed on the chart. Tell them that the chart can serve as a guide to follow during the year, and that additions can be made to it at any time.

11. Ask if anyone feels that they might have a problem abiding by the "rules" on the chart. Discuss. Stress the need for cooperation and the fact that everyone working together will make a huge difference.

12. Ask the class to sign an agreement which states, "We agree to follow the rules we created together to have a peaceful classroom." Hang this next to the "A Peaceful Classroom Is One in Which . . ." chart.

13. Copy the Peaceful Classroom chart and send it home to your students' parents with a note (suggested wording on page 51).

14. Discuss the note with your class. Ask them to discuss it and the chart rules with their families for homework.

15. Conclude by reading "Friends" (see page 52).

Lesson 1
Learning the Skills of Peacemaking

Dear Parent(s),

Our class has developed a set of rules (attached) which we have all agreed to follow throughout the year. We invite you to be our partners in the goal of having a peaceful classroom this year. Would you save these rules and talk them over with me?

Throughout the year we'll be doing other activities like this from a program called *Learning the Skills of Peacemaking*. In this program we are learning that peace starts with each individual, and that it's important for all of us to take responsibility for our actions.

If you have any questions about the program, or our rules for a peaceful classroom, my teacher would be happy to speak to you.

Thanks very much.

Child's Name

FRIENDS

by Jonathan Sprout

Have you ever travelled far away to another town?
Did you feel like a stranger when you were there?
It's just a state of mind. You can feel at home anywhere.
Anywhere you go, there are kids who care.
There are no towns full of bad people.
In every town there are good people.
And just like you and me
They wish we all were friends.
Far away in countries all around the world
There are millions of people we may never see.
But they're reaching out and they're opening up their hearts.
And they want to be friends with you and me.
There are no countries full of bad people.
In every country there are good people.
And just like you and me
They wish that we were friends.
Everywhere you look today
People want to give.
It doesn't matter what they say,
We all should live
As friends!
No matter where we live
Or what language we speak
No matter what religion we believe in
No matter how we dress
Or what lifestyle we seek
No matter the color of our skin.

RESOLVING CONFLICTS — "THE QUICK METHOD" (K-2)

OBJECTIVES

- To introduce the basics of conflict resolution.
- To guide the children to understand the benefits of resolving conflicts peacefully.

MATERIALS

- Puppets
- Chalkboard
- Chart:

> **Quick WIN/WIN**
> 1. Cool off
> 2. "I Message"
> 3. Brainstorm solutions
> 4. Affirm, forgive, thank

PROCEDURE

1. Have the children form a circle on the floor. Introduce the puppets. Tell the children that the puppets are having a disagreement or conflict over a toy that they want.

   Have the puppets act out the conflict: grab at each other, call each other names, cry, or whatever else your imagination comes up with.

2. Speak directly to the puppets. Ask each puppet to state the problem. Don't let the puppets interrupt each other. Let them know that each will get a turn.

3. Help the puppets understand others' "point of view." Teach them how to use "I Messages."

4. Ask the children to brainstorm solutions to the puppets' conflict. List all their suggestions on the board.

5. Talk to the puppets again and have them choose a solution that satisfies them both. Have the puppets thank the class for helping them work it out.

6. Have the puppets ask the children why it's better to work it out than fight it out; discuss.

7. Have the puppets ask the children about conflicts they have had. Discuss the brainstorming solutions together. Choose the most viable. Go over giving "I Messages" at this time.

8. Ask the children if they would be willing to try working out their problems this way in order to create the peaceful class they would like to have.

9. Go over the above chart with the class.

RESOLVING CONFLICTS — "THE QUICK METHOD" (3-6)

OBJECTIVES

- To introduce the basics of conflict resolution.
- To guide the children to understand the benefits of resolving conflicts peacefully.

MATERIALS

- Clipboard
- Chart of Quick "Win/Win"
- Large blank chart paper and marker

Quick WIN/WIN

1. Cool off
2. "I Message"
3. Brainstorm solutions
4. Affirm, forgive, thank

PROCEDURE

1. Introduce the lesson by staging a conflict with another staff person over an unreturned book. Have the other person storm out.

2. Students will respond. Ask for suggestions as to how to work out the conflict. Elicit as many ideas as possible. List them on large chart paper.

3. Let the children know that what they just saw was a staged conflict. Say, "In our class this year, when we have a problem with another person, instead of becoming enemies we are going to try to work things out."

4. Say, "I am going to teach you a quick way to work conflicts out. Later in our peacemaking program you will learn to work problems out in more detail." (Go over chart with class. Emphasize "I Messages." Give examples of it.)

5. Listen to conflicts the children have had and have students play act with the "quick method."

6. Say, "When you have conflicts that you can't seem to resolve yourself and I'm busy, you can list them on our clipboard. [Show and tell where it will hang.] You list the date, the names of the people involved, and briefly describe the problem. Include your signature. A number of times a week, I'll take the clipboard problems and we will help each other as a group to work them out."

7. Say, "What would our class be like if everybody was willing to talk and work out their problems?"

8. Say, "What would the world be like if government leaders did the same?"

I'M A SPECIAL AND UNIQUE PERSON

OBJECTIVES

- The children will complete "Me Mobiles" with the headings:

    1. Me

    2. My best friend

    3. My family

    4. My favorite food

    5. My favorite color

    NOTE: The teacher can write the headings ahead of time, or the children can do this when they receive their mobile papers.

- The children will learn to use the Guidelines for Sharing.

- The children will experience an increased sense of self-esteem through awareness and sharing.

- The children will understand that the statement "Peace begins with me" means, in part, feeling good about themselves.

MATERIALS

- "I Am An Individual" chart (see page 59—you can make one for each child if you wish)

- Five 5 x 7 square pieces of construction paper per child for "Me Mobile" sections (see illustration on page 60)

- Hangers, yarn scissors, hole punchers

- Crayons, markers

- Chart

GUIDELINES FOR SHARING

Treat each other with respect.

Each person listens while others are speaking.

Focus on the speaker, not your own thoughts.

Everyone waits their turn.

Don't say or do anything to put one another down.

Don't interrupt.

PROCEDURE

1. Have the children sit in a circle on the floor cross-legged.

2. Read "I Am An Individual." Explain anything the children don't understand. Discuss. Reiterate the fact that we are all special and unique. Tell the children that they will be doing a project which will focus on their specialness. Tell the children they will first learn a way to create calmness in their classroom and in themselves. Ask them to sit very still. Say: "I'm going to teach you how to breathe deeply and peacefully. Imagine your stomach is a balloon. Quietly breathe in through your nose and bring your breath all the way down to your stomach. Expand your stomach as though it's a balloon. Now quietly let the air out breathing through your nose. At the same time, deflate your stomach." Repeat this three or four times. When everyone is perfectly still say, "Listen to the quiet. Feel the calmness we have created.

3. Say, "We will be recreating this calmness often throughout the school year. The calmness helps you feel good inside. It also helps you think and learn."

   NOTE: This technique is invaluable. It can be used at the start of each day or at the start of different lessons. It can also be used at times when your class is noisy. You can stop everything for several minutes, do this technique, and then resume teaching in a more relaxed atmosphere. This technique is the one most frequently used to help children calm down when they are in conflict.

4. Say, "What is the most special thing about you? Is it something you can do like ride a bike [adapt this for older children], or the color of your hair, or a certain way you are, like kind or generous? Think about this, and we'll go around the circle and tell each other what's the most special thing about us."

5. Refer to the Guidelines for Sharing. Say, "As we take our turns, these guidelines will help us listen and speak as a group." Discuss each guideline and make sure it's understood.

6. Begin the circle discussion by saying, "The most special thing about me is." Encourage each child to share. Other children can help those who are shy or embarrassed by saying things like, "I think Janie is special because she's always nice to other people." Children who feel awkward can "pass" but should be encouraged to raise their hands later if they think of something to share.

7. Proceed around the circle. Encourage each child to finish the sentence, "The most special thing about me is ..."

8. Pass out the "Me Mobile" parts. Read and describe each heading referred to in the objectives. Write these headings on the board for the children to copy in small letters. Have the children draw an illustration for each heading.

9. Children should be encouraged to talk quietly with their neighbors about what they are drawing. This can be done at their seats, in the circle, or in small groups.

10. Display the completed mobiles in the classroom or in the halls. Discuss the mobiles together and continue to stress the specialness and uniqueness of each child. Say, "We all have a contribution to make to the world around us as the result of our specialness." Discuss the meaning of the word "contribution."

11. As a follow-up game, you can ask the children to form groups according to "favorites." For example, ask everyone whose favorite food is pizza to go to the back of the room. Then the children introduce themselves to one another. Or, have half the class pick names out of a box containing papers with names of the other half of the class in it. The children find their partners. Then they read and discuss each other's "Me Mobiles" and compare "favorites."

NOTE: Younger children (grade 1) may have some difficulty drawing the details of their favorite things early in the year, so this activity can be saved for a later time when small muscle coordination is better developed. Instead, young children can draw a large picture of "My Family and Me." Favorite things can be spoken about and listed on a chart, or a large collage can be made of "favorites" cut out from magazines. However, with older students (grades 2-6) this is an excellent activity for the first week of school.

I AM AN INDIVIDUAL

by Naomi Drew

I am an individual.
I have dignity and worth.
I am unique.
I deserve respect and I respect others.
I am part of the human family.
I have something special to offer the world.
I am committed to a peaceful world for all of us.
I make a difference, and so do you.
I can accomplish whatever I set out to do, and so can you.
I am the key to peace.

"ME" MOBILE

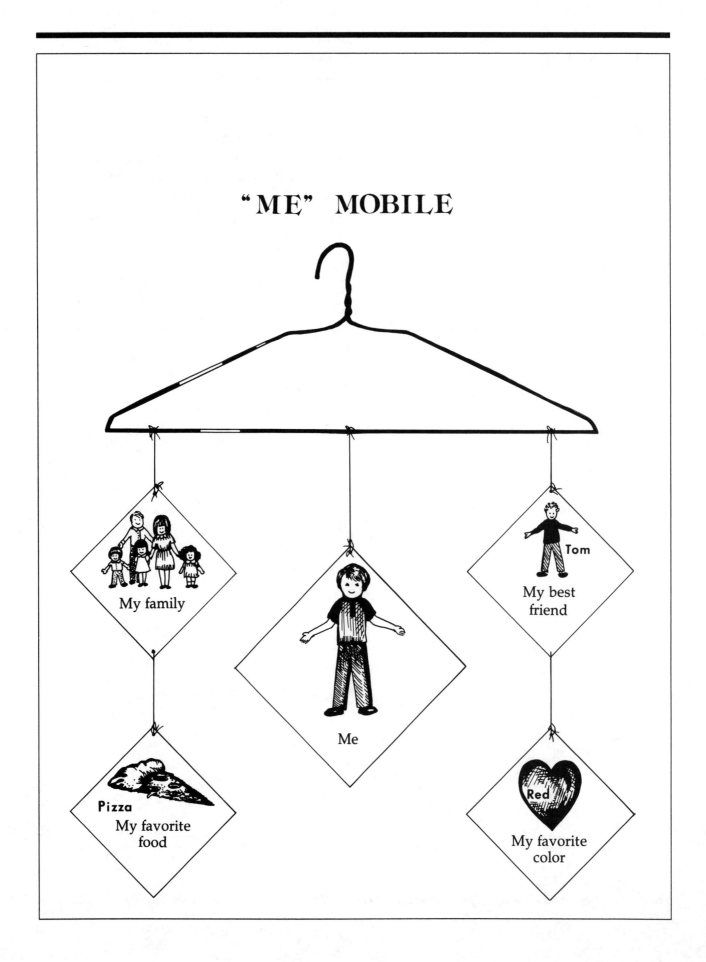

DEFINING PEACE

OBJECTIVES

- The children will explore personal meanings of peace.

- The children will learn one definition of peace: "Peace means taking care of ourselves, each other, and our earth."

- The children will learn that peace is personal but also denotes a sense of responsibility and a commitment to others and the environment.

MATERIALS

- Guidelines for Sharing

- Large paper with words written on it in bright letters: "What Peace Feels Like to Me"

- "Peace means taking care of ourselves, each other, and our earth" on a poster

- Posters or pictures from magazines showing the following:

    a. People taking care of themselves (emotional and physical well-being)

    b. People taking care of each other (love, assistance)

    c. People taking care of the earth (environment)

    Children can bring these in ahead of time.

- Posters or pictures showing the result of people not taking care of themselves, one another, the earth. Children can bring these in ahead of time.

- Drawing paper and crayons for young children. Writing paper and pencils (for older children).

    NOTE: This lesson correlates with Bulletin Board 1, entitled "Peace Means Taking Care of Ourselves, Each Other, and Our Earth."

PROCEDURE

1. Have the children sit in a circle. Go over the Guidelines for Sharing.

2. Say, "In order to create a calm and peaceful atmosphere in our classroom, we are first going to get very still and take some deep breaths. Let your body relax. Let a warm, calm, peaceful feeling flow through every part of you, from the tips of your toes to the top of your head. Listen to your own breathing. Listen to the perfect silence and calmness in our room. Now take a

moment and think about what peace feels like to you." Give students a moment of silence in which to do this.

3. Say, "What does peace feel like to you?" On the large paper entitled "What Peace Feels Like to Me," record their answers. Accept anything, but try to guide your students away from the stereotyped concepts of peace. This exercise allows students to explore their beliefs and feelings about peace.

4. Ask, "What does peace look like to you? How does this room look when it's peaceful? How does your home and the people in it look when they are peaceful? How does your street or neighborhood look when it is peaceful? How do you think our earth would look if it were peaceful?" Discuss. Encourage lots of participation. Acknowledge each child's response. Continue to guide your children away from the stereotyped meanings of peace. Allow them to draw from their own experiences of peacefulness.

5. Say, "Here is one definition of peace: 'Peace means taking care of ourselves, each other, and our earth.'" Show the sign you have made with these words on it. Be sure this is written in large, bright letters. This will serve as a sign to be displayed in the room.

6. Ask a child to read the sign aloud. Discuss.

7. Show pictures of people taking care of themselves, etc. Have the students describe what they see in the pictures. Ask, "Why is taking care of ourselves important if we want peace?" Stress this: Peace starts with the individual. Tell the students that when they take care of themselves, they are meeting their physical, emotional, and safety needs. Ask, "How do you feel when your needs are not met?" Guide students to see that when their needs are not met, they do not feel peaceful inside.

8. Show pictures depicting results of not taking care of yourself, one another, and the earth. Have students describe and discuss. Encourage full participation.

9. Ask students to draw or write about a time when they have taken care of themselves, someone else, or the environment. Have them share their pictures and stories. Allow time for discussion. Thank each child who shares.

10. Ask, "Where does peace start?" Guide the children to reiterate that peace starts with the individual. Have the children work in small groups, each child writing or drawing his or her own definition or idea of peace. Explain that the way they work together can be a peacemaking activity. Ask, "How can we be peaceful as we work together?" Encourage the sharing of ideas.

11. Have the children read or show their definitions or pictures of what they interpret peace to be. Discuss. Hang the pictures on the bulletin board, and enjoy them. Each time you need some extra peacefulness inside, look at the pictures.

Bulletin Board 1
Learning the Skills of Peacemaking

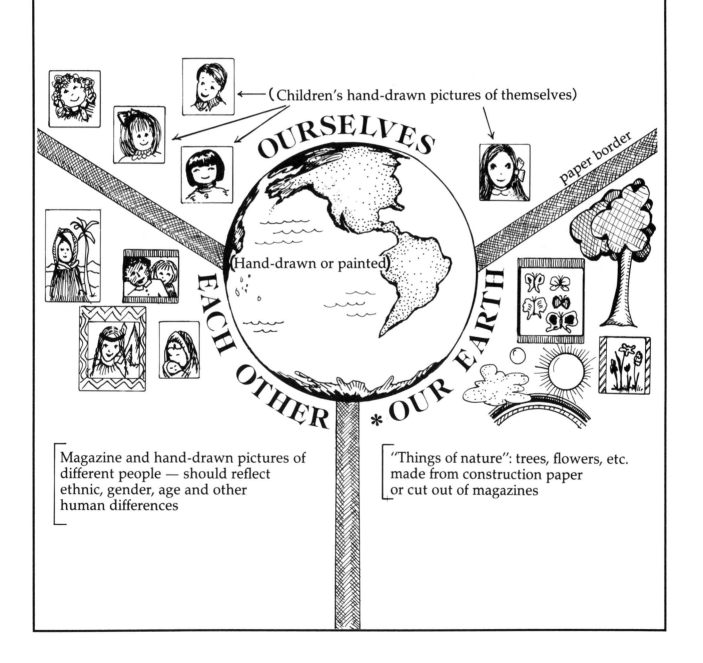

PEACE MEANS TAKING CARE OF OURSELVES, EACH OTHER, & OUR EARTH

OURSELVES

(Children's hand-drawn pictures of themselves)

paper border

(Hand-drawn or painted)

EACH OTHER

* OUR EARTH

Magazine and hand-drawn pictures of different people — should reflect ethnic, gender, age and other human differences

"Things of nature": trees, flowers, etc. made from construction paper or cut out of magazines

THE PROCESS OF AFFIRMING

OBJECTIVES

- The children will understand that peace starts with the individual, and when they affirm others they create an atmosphere of acceptance that is crucial to peacemaking.

- The children will understand and use the process of affirmation in school and at home.

MATERIALS

- Poem: "Being Human Is Being Special" (page 67)

- "The Process of Affirming" Poster:

> THE PROCESS OF AFFIRMING
>
> First, just notice what is special about the other person.
>
> Make a sincere statement to the other person about whatever is positive or special about him/ her.
>
> Be sure to look directly at the other person as you speak.
>
> Relax, and know that the other person is just like you inside.

- Paper and pencils for kids old enough to express themselves through writing; crayons and drawing paper for younger children

PROCEDURE

1. Ask the class to sit in a circle.

2. Read the poem "Being Human Is Being Special."

3. State, "Each of you is very special. I like being your teacher. I think you're great." Pause and look at your students. Ask them how they felt when you just spoke the words you did. Tell them that what you just did was to affirm them. Say, "When we affirm, we make a sincere, positive statement about another person or people."

4. Ask, "How do you feel when people affirm you?" Discuss. Don't be surprised if some students express feelings of embarrassment and awkwardness at being acknowledged. This is natural.

5. Refer to the poster: The Process of Affirming. Read it to the class. Remind the class that peace begins with each of us. When we affirm one another it creates an atmosphere of acceptance that is crucial to peacemaking. Say, "When we feel accepted by other people it becomes easier to work out our differences with them. We're all the same inside, but sometimes we forget that. Affirming helps connect us in a special way. Today we're going to learn to affirm one another. We can affirm people any time at all. The more we concentrate on the positive things about people, the easier it is to get along."

6. State, "Now we're going to have the opportunity to affirm one another in pairs. This is especially important if your partner is someone you don't usually 'hang around' with. Remember that not having peace often results from not accepting people who are different from us in some way. Boys and girls not accepting one another is a perfect example of this.

How many boys in here have felt negatively toward another person because that person happens to be a girl?" Ask for a show of hands. "How many girls have had negative feelings toward others because those people happen to be boys?" Ask for a show of hands.

7.   Say, "Peace starts with the individual and it starts with the daily decisions we make about other people. If we're committed to being peacemakers, then we must decide to focus more on likenesses than differences. We need to remember our commitment to peace even when we are faced with barriers." Explain the meaning of barriers.

8.   Say, "Now you will have an opportunity to overcome a barrier, to be a peacemaker, and to affirm someone else—even if that person isn't someone you normally play with."

9.   Say, "Turn and face the person who is sitting next to you. Each person should have a partner. Acknowledge that person by nodding your head. Remember that any negative faces or comments you might make are a put-down to that person. Be kind."

10. Say, "Now let's all take a deep breath and get very calm and relaxed. Let any negative thoughts leave you. If they come back just let them pass. Just look at the person you're sitting across from. Notice that this person has eyes, nose, mouth and hair—just like you. Realize that this person has a brain and a heart beating inside—just like you. Know that this person has the same need for love and acceptance that you have."

11. Say, "Now think of something positive about your partner. Is it his or her smile, or eyes, or is it something about the way this person acts that's positive? Affirm your partner, stating the positive quality you thought of." Allow time for the partners to affirm one another. Some might need coaching from the teacher. Every student should be encouraged to complete the affirmation.

12. Have the students face front in a circle. Ask, "How did you feel during this activity?" Discuss. Allow the feelings of awkwardness to surface, especially in older children. Encourage their honesty and candor. Affirm them for participating.

13. Now state, "I am going to affirm each of you." Go around the circle and say something positive to each child. Be careful to notice your own barriers. If you're comfortable, shake hands, or put your hand on an arm or shoulder as you speak.

> NOTE: When I did this with my class, I held both hands as I spoke to each child. It was very moving; in fact, I had to blink back tears as I looked deeply into the eyes of each of my students. A strong feeling of warmth and care connected us. It was a special moment that brought us all closer together.

14. If there's time, repeat the process with the same partners. Say, "Let's affirm our partners again." Restate the importance of affirming others. Ask the students to affirm someone when they go home.

15. Ask each student to draw an "affirmation picture" of their partner. This picture should reflect the positive quality they noticed in that person. Below the picture, older children can write the affirmation too. Example: "Billy is kind. He shares his eraser with me."

> NOTE: Depending on your class and the age of your students, you can expand affirmations to include handshaking and hugs. In my class, it eventually became very normal to see children hug one another. A wonderful experience arose out of a conflict between two of my "tough" little boys. One child asked me to mediate a conflict. I asked if he would go back to the child with whom he was having the conflict, work it out, and then affirm one another. In time I noticed the two boys talking, then shaking hands, and eventually hugging.

BEING HUMAN IS BEING SPECIAL

by Naomi Drew

I look in the mirror and who do I see.
My very own person who looks just like me.
I look at my eyes, I look at my face,
Knowing that no one on earth or in space
Is quite like I am, one of a kind.
My body is special and so is my mind.
Each person alive has something special to give.
We each make a difference each day that we live.
I love myself and I love others too.
The world is a special place,
'Cause it has me and you.

DEFINING CONFLICT RESOLUTION

OBJECTIVES

- The children will understand the definition of conflict resolution.
- The children will understand and describe a conflict they have experienced in the classroom, with peers, or outside.
- The children will think about a solution to their conflict.

MATERIALS

- Chart for teacher to record children's responses, entitled "Conflict Words/Conflict Resolution Words"

PROCEDURE

1. Ask the children to form a discussion circle, and ask, "What is a conflict?" Discuss.

2. Say, "A conflict is a fight, a disagreement, or a problem. It usually involves more than one person. Often people become angry during a conflict. Conflict resolution is solving the problem so no one loses, and so that physical force is not used. When we resolve a conflict successfully, both sides feel like their needs have been met."

3. Say, "Today I want you to think of a specific conflict you have had that you weren't able to work out."

4. Allow the children to briefly share their conflicts aloud. Go around the circle and ask each child to make a statement. Example: "My friend and I had a fight over which game we should play during recess." Caution the children not to discuss anything too personal or to use names. Encourage each child in the room to share, stressing that conflict is a natural part of relationships. State, "We all have conflicts at one time or another. Anger is a natural feeling. There are ways of expressing our anger that work and there are ways that don't work." Explain "not working" as things we do which end up making matters worse, or don't help to resolve the conflict. Say, "Today we'll be thinking about ways that 'work.' In describing our conflict, think about how you 'worked things out' with the other person or if you worked

them out at all. Solutions that work satisfy both sides. These solutions are called 'Win/Win.'"

5. Say, "In order for a conflict to be resolved, at least one person needs to be committed to finding a solution that works." Ask the children to think of a time they worked something out with another person when both people felt satisfied in the end. Discuss.

6. Give a personal example.

7. Ask, "Have you ever worked out a conflict with someone who wasn't committed to working it out? Do you think it's possible to resolve a conflict when you are the only one committed to doing so?" Give a personal example of a conflict you worked out, even when the other person wasn't committed.

8. Have the children sit in a circle. Say, "We're going to relax and think of a time we had a conflict. Take a deep breath, allowing a warm, relaxed feeling to come over you. Take several more breaths and feel the quietness in our room. Now think about a conflict you have had recently. Think of the words you spoke and the feelings you had when you were angry. Think of the words the other person spoke. Now think of a better way the conflict could have been resolved. Think of a solution. Think about what you and the other person are saying to solve the problem. Think about how your bodies are moving, your facial expressions and the room

you are in. Think of both of you working out the problem. Think of the other person's face. Now, think of your own. Try to feel the other person's feelings. What words are you speaking to bring about your solution? Think of yourself happy and satisfied."

9. Have the children discuss the conflicts and solutions they thought about.

10. Ask the children to return to their seats. Pass out paper and have the children write "My Conflict" on one side, and "My Solution" on the other. Have them illustrate their conflict and solutions. They can write descriptions also.

11. After the children have drawn, or written, ask them to describe the pictures they have drawn of their conflicts and perceived solutions. Ask them to state what they said in the conflict situation and in the solution of it.

12. As each child gives an example, ask, "What did you say when you were angry? What did you say when you were solving the problem?" Record key phrases on the chart you have prepared entitled, "Conflict Words/Conflict Resolution Words." Example:

CONFLICT WORDS

(Example:)

"You'd better give me back my book right now!"

CONFLICT RESOLUTION WORDS

(Example:)

"Let's share the book until you find yours."

---

13. Guide the children to notice the distinction between the conflict words and the conflict resolution words. Help them to see that conflict words express anger and judgment. They close doors to communication. Conflict phrases often start with the word "you." On the other hand, conflict resolution words often denote compromise and conciliation. They open the doors. Often people ask questions and look for solutions when they use conflict resolution words.

14. Tell the children that it's hard for people to resolve conflicts when they are angry. Sometimes we need time to cool off first. Say, "In another lesson we're going to learn a set of guidelines which will help us resolve conflicts so each person wins. We'll talk about other conflicts we have had and ways we can solve them."

15. Say, "Take your papers home and share them with your families. Tell them what you discovered today about conflicts and solutions."

WHAT GETS IN THE WAY OF RESOLVING CONFLICTS

OBJECTIVES

- The children will reiterate the meaning of conflict and conflict resolution.

- The children will understand how they usually handle conflicts.

- The children will understand what emotions and thoughts impair their ability or willingness to resolve conflicts peacefully.

- The children will understand that they have choices in the way they resolve conflicts.

MATERIALS

- Story, "Michael's Bad Morning" (see below)

- Chalkboard, chalk

- Chart: Conflict Words/Conflict Resolution Words from Lesson 7

PROCEDURE

1. Have the children sit in a circle.

2. Tell them that they're going to hear a short story about a boy named Michael who has a fight at the bus stop. Say, "As you listen to the story, think about what caused the conflict, and how Michael felt."

3. Read: "Michael's Bad Morning."

MICHAEL'S BAD MORNING

It was Monday morning. Michael didn't want to get up and go to school. His bed felt so warm and inviting and it was cold outside. He opened his eyes slowly and noticed his dog, Prowler, lying on the floor chewing his brand new sneaker. "Prowler, get out of here!" he yelled angrily. Prowler ran off and hid in a corner.

He rose, slowly dressed, brushed his teeth and went downstairs, doubly angry because one of his new sneakers was ruined, plus he had to go to school today. "Why couldn't it still be Sunday?" he thought.

Michael ate breakfast, got his book bag, and went to the bus stop. The kids were playing kickball. As he bent over to put his book bag down, the ball flew over and popped him in the head. "Ouch!" he yelled. "Who did that?"

It was Tommy who guiltily called out, "I didn't mean it, really," as the other kids laughed. Michael exploded.

"Oh yes you did, you dummy. See if you like the way it feels!" And with that, he lifted the ball and threw it back at Tommy, hitting him in the stomach.

Tommy yelled out, "Hey, that's not fair. The ball hit you by accident, but you did that on purpose. You're mean." This time Tommy threw the ball hard at Michael's leg. Next, the two boys were fighting.

---

4. Ask, "What caused the fight?" Discuss. Encourage the children to air their reactions.

5. Ask, "How would you have handled the situation if you were Michael, at the moment the ball hit you in the head?" Discuss.

6. Ask, "What got in the way of working out the problem?"

7. Ask, "Do you ever feel so angry you don't want to work out a problem?" Discuss and ask for examples. You can give your own personal example.

8. Ask, "What are some of the other choices Michael had, rather than throwing the ball back

at Tommy?" Discuss, and list the children's responses on the board under the heading "Other Choices." Some might be:

- Yell, but don't hurt the other person. Walk away until you've calmed down and then tell the person how you felt.
- Throw the ball hard in another direction so it doesn't hurt anyone.
- See the humor in the situation.

Allow the responses to come from the children, but guide them to see that there are choices. Encourage them to come up with as many as possible.

9. Say, "Think of a time when you were angry and you didn't want to work it out. Turn to the person you are sitting next to and tell him or her about it. Take turns." Have the children share for several minutes.

10. Ask, "Who would like to tell the class about a conflict you have had that you didn't want to work out?" Again, remind the children not to share anything too personal and not to use real names. As each child shares, ask the question, "What got in the way of working it out?"

11. Ask, "What other choices did you have that you might not have been aware of?" Have the children turn to their partners and discuss. Next have them share as a group.

12. Say, "Even though you generally have choices in the way you handle conflicts, sometimes you might not be aware of those choices because you're too angry or upset. That's part of being human, and it doesn't mean you're bad. The thing to remember is to stop and think each time you have a conflict, and see if there's a different way you might handle it, so that in the end, the problem isn't worse." Discuss.

13. Say, "In the next lesson, you're going to learn about 'I messages' which will help you work out conflicts."

USING "I MESSAGES"

NOTE: Refer to *Parent Effectiveness Training,* by Thomas Gordon, or *Effectiveness Training for Women,* by Linda Evans, before doing this lesson. Giving "I Messages" is a complex communication technique. These books will help.

OBJECTIVES

- The children will act out problems that lead to conflict.
- The children will learn to use "I Messages" in conflict situations.

MATERIALS

- "I Messages/You Messages" poster

I MESSAGES

I feel angry.

I'm sad because you took my toy.

I'm embarrassed because you called me a name.

YOU MESSAGES

You're a pain.

You're mean.

You make me mad.

PROCEDURE

1. Have the children sit in a circle. Have them take several deep breaths until they feel relaxed and quiet. Have them listen to the silence in the room.

2. Say, "Today we're going to talk about something you can do that will help you work out your differences when you have a conflict."

3. Say, "We talked briefly about giving 'I messages' when the quick method of Win/Win was introduced. Today we're going to go over this in more depth. There are two ways people can speak when they are talking about their feelings. People can start either with the word 'I' or 'You.'"

4. Say, "When you start with the word 'I' you don't place blame on others. 'I Messages' show that you are responsible for the way you feel. When you start with the word 'I' you don't put

the other person on the defensive." Explain. Say "Remember, we all are responsible for our own feelings." Discuss.

5. Ask the students to look at the chart with "I/You Messages." Have a student read it aloud. Explain that "You Messages" put other people on the defensive and make them less likely to want to solve conflicts.

6. Relate the following conflict situations one at a time. After each one, have the children first respond with a "You Message," and then an "I Message."

    a. Janice cuts in front of Sarah in line.

    Sarah responds with the following "You Message" (children's responses).

    Next have a child turn Sarah's "You Message" into an "I Message."

b. Candace accidentally spills Anthony's milk at lunchtime.

Anthony's "You Message" (children's responses).

Have a child change Anthony's "You Message" into an "I Message."

c. Julio gets an A on his math test. Josh, who got a D, calls Julio a nerd.

Julio gives the following "You Message" (children's responses).

Have a child turn Julio's "You Message" into an "I Message."

7. Students will act out the following situations, first as they would normally handle it, then using "I Messages."

a. There is a pencil on the floor. Two people go to pick it up at once. They start to argue over whose pencil it is.

b. Tom and Jason are walking to lunch. Mike asks if he can join them. Tom and Jason ignore Mike. Mike feels hurt.

c. Maria and Peggy are working on a project together. Peggy hasn't brought the materials she is responsible for. Now the project might have to be turned in late.

d. Alan's friend yelled at him this morning on the playground. Alan comes to school sad and upset. When another friend, Dave, says hello to him in line, Alan says, "Get out of here!"

After each scenario, discuss what worked better, the "old way" or using "I Messages."

NOTE: Giving "I Messages" is tricky. You'll need to have your students practice this quite a few times before they get the hang of it.

8. Come up with other situations where the children can practice using "I Messages." Give them time to practice.

9. Ask, "How do you suppose this could work with countries who don't get along?"

10. Ask, "How do you think it's possible for nations to work out their differences through talking to one another?"

11. Ask, "Do you think it's worth the extra effort for nations to try this? Why?"

NOTE: Here's a way to generate some extra enthusiasm about giving "I Messages." Keep a medium-sized jar and a supply of pennies on your desk. Every time a child gives an "I Message" to someone, he gets to drop a penny in the jar. When the jar is filled, the class gets to have a pizza party.

WIN/WIN GUIDELINES

OBJECTIVES

- The children will state the definitions of conflict and conflict resolution.

- The children will understand that conflict is a normal occurrence in relationships, yet positive choices can be made in response to conflict.

- The children will learn the full Win/Win Guidelines as a way to solve conflicts peacefully.

MATERIALS

- Copies of Win/Win Guidelines and Abbreviated Win/Win Guidelines for the students to take home.

- Chart displaying the Win/Win Guidelines (see page 77)

- Chart displaying Abbreviated Win/Win Guidelines (page 78)

- Chart displaying Rules for Using Win/Win Guidelines (page 79)

PROCEDURE

1. State, "We have talked about conflicts we've had with people in our lives. Is it okay to have conflicts? Do all people have conflicts at one time or another?" Ask, "Is it possible to solve conflicts without hurting each other through our words or actions? When both people feel good at the end of a conflict, that is called Win/Win."

2. Say, "Today we are going to learn some guidelines that will help us deal with conflicts in such a way that both partners feel good, and so that no one loses."

3. Show the Win/Win Guidelines and the Abbreviated Guidelines on the charts. It works well to have each guideline in a different color. Ask several students to read one guideline at a time. Remind the children that this is the complete version of the Quick Method they learned in lesson 2 and 3.

4. Discuss each guideline. Ask what each guideline means to the students. Ask if they have been using the Quick Method. Ask if it worked. Discuss.

5. Discuss the word "commitment." Remind students that a commitment is a promise one makes to oneself or someone else that is kept no matter what. Say, "Often we don't keep our promises when we are challenged too much.

Commitment means that you keep your promise, regardless." State, "When at least one party in a conflict is committed to working the problem out, then it is possible to use the Win/Win Guidelines successfully."

6. Ask, "If you have had a conflict with another person, and you're both angry, and then that other person calls you a name, should you stop being committed to working it out?" "What if the other person isn't committed to working it out? Should you decide not to be committed, too?" Discuss.

7. Ask, "Who does peace start with? Why is it important to keep your commitments?" Stress that there are times when it is difficult to be a peacemaker. Sometimes it is lonely to be the only one willing to work it out. Ask, "If we want to have a peaceful world, is it worth facing difficulties and sometimes working out the problem even if it's hard to do?" Discuss. Stress that peace starts with the commitment of individuals. Mention committed peacemakers—like Martin Luther King, Corazon Aquino, Rosa Parks, and Gandhi—who stood up for their beliefs even when they had little support.

8. Ask, "How do you think the countries of the world would get along if they were committed to working things out peacefully?"

IMPORTANT NOTE: The next step should be repeated at least once a week throughout the year. Also, don't forget to use the Win/Win Guidelines to "showcase," as described in the chapter "Creating a Peaceful School."

9. Say, "Now we're going to act out some conflict situations. Remember, we always have a choice when conflicts arise. We can choose positive or negative actions. But when we choose the negatives there's often a negative consequence." Discuss.

a. Go over Rules for Using Win/Win Guidelines. Make sure everyone fully understands them.

b. Distribute copies of the Win/Win Guidelines.

c. Ask the students if anyone has a real conflict which they would like to act out with others in the class. Allow several students to describe their conflicts. Choose one conflict to re-enact.

d. Have the student describe the particular conflict. Do not use the real names of people involved. Children can say, "my friend" or "someone I know."

e. Choose students to play the different parts. Have the student whose conflict it is quietly and briefly go over the "parts" with the players.

f. Ask the players to go to the center of the circle and act out the conflict as it was, including the way in which it was actually concluded.

g. Discuss the feelings of the participants. Discuss why the outcome didn't work. Ask, "Who lost?"

h. Now replay the conflict using the Win/Win Guidelines. Guide the students through each stage. It is the role of the teacher to coach the students each time they play act using the Win/Win Guidelines. You do not have to have your students memorize them. Instead, through repeated play acting, coaching and reinforcement, they will eventually assimilate the Guidelines.

i. Discuss the Win/Win simulation. How did the players feel? Ask, "What are the advantages to using Win/Win Guidelines?"

j. Homework: "Tell your family about the Win/Win Guidelines." Say, "Hang them up where everyone in the house can see them. Ask your family if they will try using the guidelines in their next conflict."

NOTE: Here's something really effective you can do to teach and reinforce the Win/Win Guidelines. Have children from the upper grades (3-6) go to the lower grades (K-2) to help introduce and practice the Win/Win strategies. Both age groups love it and they all profit by continued practice of these vital skills.

THE WIN/WIN GUIDELINES

1. Take time for cooling off if needed. Find alternative ways to express anger.

2. Each person states their feelings and the problem as they see it, using "I Messages." No blaming, no name-calling, no interrupting.

3. Each person states the problem as the *other person* sees it.*

4. Each person says how they themselves are responsible for the problem.*

5. Brainstorm solutions together and choose a solution that satisfies both — a Win/Win solution.

6. Affirm, forgive, or thank.

*Optional Steps.

ABBREVIATED WIN/WIN GUIDELINES

1. Cool off

2. "I Message"

3. Say back

4. Take responsibility

5. Brainstorm solutions

6. Affirm, forgive, or thank

RULES FOR USING WIN/WIN GUIDELINES

1. Be respectful toward each other.

2. Listen while the other person speaks.

3. Be honest.

4. No blaming, name-calling, interrupting.

5. Work toward a solution both people are comfortable with.

WHAT ELSE CAN I DO?

OBJECTIVES

- The children will determine what their reactions are when they get angry.
- The children will look at the choices they usually make when they get angry.
- The children will understand the meaning of "consequences."
- The children will look at what other choices they can make when they get angry.

MATERIALS

- Chalkboard, chalk
- Worksheets (page 83), one for each child, and pencils
- Large chart paper for brainstorming
- Marker
- Peacemaking Logs (a compositon notebook is fine)

PROCEDURE

1. Have the children form a circle. Tell them an anecdote about a time you got really angry. Describe your physical sensations (heart racing, etc.) and how they made you feel.

Tell the class how you chose to handle your anger. You don't need to pick an incident where you were pleased with the way you handled yourself. It might even be better to tell them about a time when your anger got the best of you. Let them see that we are all challenged by angry feelings, and we all can learn something about dealing with this part of ourselves. Discuss your story.

2. Ask a child to share with the class a time they felt really angry. As the incident is described, list the child's responses on the board in the following categories:

- My feelings
- What I chose to do
- This was the outcome of my choice
- What else could I have chosen to do?

3. Remind the class that we always have choices when there's a conflict. Sometimes our choices result in negative outcomes. Discuss this in depth and let the class give a variety of examples of negative outcomes (loss of a friend, detention, etc.)

4. Tell the children they're going to talk with a partner about a time when they got really angry, and that they'll be listing their responses on worksheets with the same categories that have been outlined on the board.

5. Pass out the worksheets. Go over them briefly.

6. Have each child turn to the person they are sitting next to and begin sharing about a time they really got angry. As the children share, they should be filling in their worksheets.

7. After about five or so minutes, have the children re-form their circle. Ask different people to share. Guide the class in noticing similarities among reactions and outcomes.

8. List on the board some of the outcomes, like hitting or name-calling, encountered when people in the class have made a negative choice. Talk about the issue of consequences. Introduce the term if they are unfamiliar with it. Stress the fact that there are consequences for our actions.

9. Now it's time to brainstorm. Ask the class to think about the angry feelings they just talked about with their partners. Ask them to brainstorm answers to the following question:

"What else could you have done when you felt so angry?"

10. Try to fill the chart with as many ideas as possible. In essence, you're getting the class to come up with cooling off techniques they can use when they're confronted with an actual conflict. Hang this chart in the room so the children can refer to it for cooling off techniques.

11. Have the class write in their peacemaking logs about what kind of choice they will think about making next time they feel really angry. Have them explore what they need to do to calm down and avoid making a negative choice when they are angry.

WORKSHEET: WHAT ELSE CAN I DO?
Learning the Skills of Peacemaking
Lesson 11

1. When I got really angry, I felt this way in my body
   (list every reaction you can think of and describe):

2. This is what I chose to do when I felt that way:

3. This is what happened when I made that choice:

4. This is what else I could have done instead:

REFLECTIVE LISTENING

OBJECTIVES

- The children will utilize the technique of reflective listening to solve problems.

- The children will gain a deeper understanding of the importance of listening to others.

   NOTE: This lesson will prepare children to do Step 3 in the Win/Win Guidelines: "Each person states the problem as the other person sees it."

MATERIALS

- Win/Win Guidelines

- Reflective Listening Poster:

> ### REFLECTIVE LISTENING
>
> Reflective listening is listening with complete attention to the person speaking and repeating back in your own words what they just said. When people are listened to in this way they feel affirmed, and they listen better to you when it's your turn to speak.

- Paper, pencils, crayons

PROCEDURE

1. Ask the students to sit in a circle. Say, "Let's start off with some deep breathing. Bring a feeling of relaxation inside of yourself. Let that feeling help you to be calm and better able to listen, because today's lesson is about a special way of listening called reflective listening."

2. Say, "Reflective listening is something that we'll be doing when we do the Win/Win Guidelines." Go over the guidelines briefly and then direct the children's attention to Step 3: "Each person states the problem as the other person sees it." Say, "Today's lesson will help us to do that through a new way of listening. We also call reflective listening 'saying back.'"

3. Ask, "How do you feel when someone listens to you?" Discuss.

4. Show the "Reflective Listening" poster. Have a number of students read it aloud to the group.

5. Say, "Now we're going to practice reflective listening."

6. Say, "Each of us is going to have a chance to listen and be listened to. Learning reflective lis-

tening is like learning to ride a bike. At first it feels unfamiliar and may be a little hard. The more you do it the more natural it becomes, until it's part of your life." Pick a volunteer to help you model reflective listening. It's helpful to start with the words, "I heard you say..." when you begin to reflect back what you heard. Have the children do this, too.

7. Ask your volunteer to tell you what he/she likes to do best after school. Repeat back in your own words what the student said. Next, tell the student your favorite thing to do after school and have him/her repeat it back. Choose one or two more volunteers and repeat this process before going on to the next one.

8. PROCESS A: "We're going to do two processes using reflective listening. Turn to a person next to you. One of you will be 'one' and the other 'two.' 'One' will begin by telling 'two' his or her favorite things to do. When I say time, 'two' will repeat it back. Begin." Then switch roles, having "two" tell and "one" repeat back.

9. Ask, "How did it feel to be listened to fully?" Discuss. "Did you prefer listening or

being listened to?" Discuss. "How do you think reflective listening can help in working out our conflicts?"

10. PROCESS B: Say, "Now I'm going to ask a question that I want everyone to think about. We're going to go around the circle and everyone will answer the question, but before they do, they must repeat what the person before them said."

EXAMPLE: Ask the question, "Should kids get homework? Why or why not?" The teacher answers the question first: "Yes, kids should get homework because it helps them learn." Amy is next in the circle. She turns to the teacher, looks directly at the teacher, and says, "I heard you say you think kids should get homework because it helps them learn." At this point the teacher says, "Yes" because Amy reflected the statement correctly. If Amy had not, the teacher would have said, "No," and Amy would have had to try again. Now, Amy gets to give her answer to the question. She says, "No, kids shouldn't get homework because it's boring." Jason is sitting next to

her so he has to reflect back what Amy said before giving his answer. Continue around the circle until each child has had a turn to both reflect what the previous person has said and to give his/her own response.

11. After each child has spoken, discuss the process with the group. Ask, "Was it easy or hard to reflect back what someone else said?"

12. Say, "Knowing reflective listening will help us do Step 3 of the Win/Win Guidelines, where you state how your partner feels."

13. Follow-up activity: children respond in writing to the following questions. How does it feel when someone really listens to me? Why is it important to listen to others? Young children can draw a picture which expresses how they feel when they are truly listened to.

NOTE: Repeat the reflective listening exercise as often as possible, using different questions that children can answer and reflect back to one another. You can also play the game "Why Are You Mad at Me?" (page 39, #7) for extra practice.

COOPERATIVE GROUP SIMULATIONS

OBJECTIVES

- The children will work in cooperative groups to help each other resolve conflicts.
- The children will practice using the Win/Win Guidelines and Rules for Using Win/Win.

MATERIALS

- "Cooperative Group Mediation" (page 34)
- "Cooperative Group Simulations" (pp. 37 -38)
- Transparency of Cooperative Group Simulations 1 (see Appendix)
- Overhead projector
- Chart of the Win/Win Guidelines
- Chart of Rules for Using Win/Win
- Paper and pencil for each group
- Teacher's notepad and clipboard
- Optional: Observation Record Sheet (page 36)

PROCEDURE

1. Have the children sit in a circle. Tell them they'll be playing a game in which they will take turns helping each other work out a conflict. Tell them that some people will have the opportunity to be mediator. Explain this term.

2. Refer to the chart of the Win/Win Guidelines and Abbreviated Win/Win. Go over these charts, making sure the children understand each step.

3. Refer to Rules for Using Win/Win. Go over each step.

4. Have the children get into groups of four. Refer to your Cooperative Group Mediation guide and proceed as outlined in this section. Do only one play act today, making sure the children fully understand the process.

5. Repeat this lesson once a week for at least five weeks, using the role simulation listed in the Cooperative Group Simulation section. You can make up your own simulations based on conflicts that commonly arise in your school.

The more you have the children practice this process the better. You'll see that as they practice resolving conflicts through simulations it will become more natural for them to apply the skill when actual conflicts arise in their lives.

CREATIVE BRAINSTORMING

OBJECTIVES

- The children will apply the process of brainstorming.

- The children will understand that brainstorming is a creative process that has limitless applications.

- The children will be able to apply this process later, as it applies to the Win/Win Guidelines.

MATERIALS

- A pencil
- Rules for Brainstorming Poster:

RULES FOR BRAINSTORMING

1. Say anything that comes to mind.

2. Don't judge your ideas or the ideas of others.

3. Don't limit your ideas by trying to have them make sense. Invite your mind to be absolutely creative.

4. Allow your thoughts to come quickly. Let them flow.

5. Know that people use only a small part of their brains. Brainstorming enables you to unlock the parts you don't ordinarily use. Surprise yourself with new ideas.

6. See how many creative ideas and solutions you can come up with, and don't restrict your thoughts in any way.

7. Be outrageous and have fun!

- Chart paper—A large sheet for each group of four or five children

- Markers

    NOTE: Younger children will need the assistance of one aide or helper for each group to record brainstorming ideas.

PROCEDURE

1. State, "We've talked about conflict and conflict resolution. Can you restate what a conflict is?" Discuss. "What does conflict resolution mean?" Discuss. "Is conflict a normal part of human interaction? Do we have a choice in the way we manage our conflicts?" Discuss. "Do you think it's possible to work out differences even if the other person isn't committed to doing so?" Discuss.

2. Say, "Part of working out differences is coming up with ideas for solutions that satisfy all people involved. One way to do this is through the process of brainstorming." Ask if

anyone has ever done brainstorming. If so, ask them to explain the process. If not, tell the class that brainstorming is a creative thought process in which people come up with as many ideas as possible for a topic.

3.   Say, "Today we're going to engage in a class brainstorming exercise, and the purpose will be to come up with as many uses as possible for a pencil. The rules for brainstorming are listed on this poster." Hold up the poster and go over the rules carefully.

4.   Hold up a pencil, "I want you to think of all the different possible uses for this pencil. Your answers can be silly, outrageous, realistic, unrealistic, common sense, nonsensical, useful, or useless. The whole point is not to limit your thinking. Any thought or idea that comes to you is okay."

5.   Say, "We're going to divide into groups of four or five for this process. Choose a group leader [this is where your helper is needed] who will record everybody's responses on chart paper that I will hand out." Pass out paper and markers. "Remember, don't make fun of anyone else's ideas. Everything is acceptable. Also,

you're going to have to think fast. I'm going to give you only four minutes. Try to come up with as many ideas as you can. Any questions?"

> NOTE: Younger children can do this as a class activity with the teacher recording brainstorming ideas.

6.   Time the activity. Give the class exactly four minutes. At the end, have each group leader read the complete list.

7.   Discuss the process. Note if the children's thinking shifted out of the realm of the conventional. Acknowledge this, and let them know that brainstorming holds the key to solutions for many different problems and challenges. Say, "There are limitless possibilities that the process of brainstorming unlocks."

8.   Ask, "What are some of the different ways we can use brainstorming?" Discuss.

9.   Say, "Brainstorming helps us think of solutions to conflicts where we think there are very few, or even none."

10. Say, "How can our world leaders use this process?" Discuss.

BRAINSTORMING SOLUTIONS TO CONFLICTS

OBJECTIVES

- The children will think of various conflict situations and describe them.
- The children will apply the brainstorming technique to generate possible solutions to conflict situations.
- The children will apply the Win/Win Guidelines.

MATERIALS

- Rules for Brainstorming poster (see Lesson 14)
- Chart paper for recording students' brainstorming suggestions
- Charts: Win/Win Guidelines, Abbreviated Win/Win Guidelines, and Rules for Using Win/Win Guidelines (pages 77, 78, 79)

PROCEDURE

1. Have the children form a circle. Say, "Today we're going to focus on personal conflicts and we're going to use the process of brainstorming to come up with as many possible solutions as we can."

2. Ask, "Who has had a conflict they would like to discuss with the class? Remember not to use anyone's full name or to discuss anything that is too personal."

3. Select a few children to describe their conflicts.

4. Choose one conflict on which to focus.

5. Ask the children to play act the conflict as it was.

6. Now "re-play" the conflict, using the Win/Win Guidelines. Stop when you get to "brainstorm solutions." Have the players sit down.

7. Ask the entire class to generate as many solutions as possible. Write them down on chart paper.

8. After you have exhausted every possibility, guide the children to choose several solutions.

Circle them on the chart. Encourage the class to be creative with these solutions by either combining them or suggesting their use in different ways.

9. Have the class vote on one solution. Write it on the board.

10. Remind the class that conflict resolution is a creative effort. Say, "Sometimes we don't see the solution to a conflict right away. Problem solving takes time, creativity, and the willingness to come up with ideas we wouldn't ordinarily think of."

NOTE: This process can be repeated in a condensed version several times a week. Take ten minutes at the end of the day, and generate solutions to conflicts within the room. You'll be amazed at how engaged the class becomes in the process. Bring the Win/Win Guidelines and Rules for Brainstorming to a faculty meeting. Offer your colleagues the opportunity to work out their differences using these techniques. They'll thank you.

TAKING CARE OF OUR EARTH

OBJECTIVES

- Children will actively demonstrate "peace means taking care of our earth," by cleaning up their school yard and planting flower bulbs.

- The children will understand that we are all responsible for taking care of the world around us; each person who takes responsibility makes a big difference even if it's on a small scale.

MATERIALS

- Sign: "Peace Means Taking Care of Ourselves, Each Other, and Our Earth"

- Large poster to be filled in during this lesson, entitled "Ways We Can Take Care of Our Earth"

- Trash bags, a flower bulb for each child, and old spoons or gardening shovels. If there is no yard around your school, use flower pots or window boxes.

- A picture of the type of flower that will grow from the bulbs (optional)

PROCEDURE

1. Have the children sit in a circle. Say, "Earlier, we learned how to affirm one another by telling each other something special about one another. Today we're going to affirm the earth by taking care of it in a special way." Refer to the sign "Peace means…"

2. Ask, "What does it mean to take care of our earth?" Discuss.

3. Ask, "How can we take care of our earth? Can you think of some different ways we can do this?" List the children's answers on the chart entitled "Ways We Can Take Care of Our Earth."

4. Ask the children how they can take care of the area around their school. Discuss.

5. Say, "How would our neighborhood look if everyone took care of it?" Discuss.

6. Say, "How would the world be if everyone all over took care of it? How might it be different?" Discuss.

7. Say, "Today we're going to take care of the area around our school by cleaning it up and planting flower bulbs." Show the bulbs and utensils. Show the picture of the flowers that will grow from the bulbs. Take the children outside.

8. Pass out the bulbs and trash bags. Have the children work in groups to clean and plant.

9. After you're finished, come back inside and plan your spring planting project. Have the children decide what they're going to plant in the spring (vegetables, flowers, trees).

10. Pick a date on which to do your spring planting and clean-up. Mark it on the calendar.

11. Ask the children how they like taking care of their earth. Ask why it's important to do this. Ask how the children are making a contribution by taking care of the earth. Acknowledge them for doing so.

TAKING CARE OF PEOPLE IN OUR COMMUNITY

NOTE: Prior to this lesson, arrange for a representative from a senior citizen home to speak to the class.

OBJECTIVES

- The children will meet and talk to the representative of a senior citizens' home or center in your community.

- The children will find out ways they can help the senior citizens of your community.

- The children will determine a course of action they can take as a group to work with the senior citizens.

MATERIALS

- Pamphlets or brochures from a local senior citizens' center and pictures of some of the seniors from that center, if possible.

- Chart paper (to be filled in later) entitled "Our Project for the Senior Citizens' Center" (you can put in the actual name of the center).

PROCEDURE

1. Have the children sit in a circle. Introduce the representative from the senior citizens' center.

2. Have each child introduce him/herself by going around the circle.

3. Ask the representative to tell the children about the center and those who attend or live at the center. Brochures can be passed out at this time.

4. Allow the children to ask questions. They may also want to talk about their own grandparents or other seniors they know.

5. Ask the representative to tell the children about ways they might be helpful to the people in the center. Have the children give their own suggestions.

6. Ask, "How can the senior citizens be helpful to us?" Discuss this and allow the children to come up with suggestions too. Guide the children to see that as people grow older they have a valuable contribution to make to others, especially by virtue of their knowledge and experience. Let them know that in some cultures, older people are revered.

7. Together, pick a project that the children can do with the senior citizens. The project can be mutually helpful, such as inviting a senior into the class to give extra help to those who need it. At the same time, the children can write letters to "Senior Pen Pals," letting them know about their school, families, and the peacemaking program they are involved in. If your school will allow it, make arrangements every so often for the children to visit the senior citizens' home. They can read to the senior citizens and the seniors can read to them. Or they can bake a treat and bring it in to share. There are many things you can do. Have the children decide, and fill in the chart paper "Our Project for the Senior Citizens' Center."

8. Write a note home to the children's parents (or have the children do this) and tell them about your project.

9. Ask the children how this project reflects the definition of peace they learned, "Peace means taking care of ourselves, each other, and our earth."

TAKING CARE OF THOSE WHO ARE HUNGRY

NOTE: This lesson should be done before Thanksgiving

OBJECTIVES

- The children will learn that there are many hungry people in the world, and that they can help.

- The children will understand that having a peaceful world means taking care of one another, not just oneself.

- The children will plan a mini-food drive to collect non-perishables for families who would otherwise not have enough to eat at Thanksgiving.

MATERIALS

- A current events article dealing with the issue of hunger for you to read to the class.

- Poster: "Peace Means Taking Care of Ourselves, Each Other, and Our Earth."

- Letter to parents (see page 98).

PROCEDURE

1. Have the children form a circle. Say, "Imagine getting up in the morning and not having any food to eat. You get to school and you are hungry but you don't want to tell your teacher about it. You try to do your work but you can't concentrate. You feel tired, and you wish you could put your head down. Lunch time comes, and there's still nothing for you to eat. Your stomach begins to hurt. All you can think about is food but there isn't any."

2. Give the children about three minutes of silence to imagine this. Say, "How did you feel thinking about this?" Discuss. Be especially sensitive to those children in your class who may have experienced or are experiencing feelings similar to those described in the process.

3. Tell the children that there are many hungry people in the world and the majority of them are children.

> NOTE: The Hunger Project has an excellent school in-service program. If you would like an in-depth presentation on ending hunger for your class, you can arrange for a presentation by writing the following address: The Hunger Project, 15 East 26th Street, New York, NY 10010.

4. Tell the children that hunger does not have to exist, and that they can begin to alleviate it right in their own communities.

5. Ask the children what they would like to do to help end hunger in their community. Discuss.

6. Read the current events article on hunger. Discuss it.

7. Ask the class to begin collecting canned and dry goods to be given to hungry people at Thanksgiving. You can arrange for the food to be distributed (and possibly even picked up) through one of your local churches or civic organizations.

8. Refer to the poster "Peace Means Taking Care of Ourselves, Each Other and Our Earth." Ask the children how their involvement in ending hunger relates to the words on the poster. Discuss.

9. Distribute the letters to parents. Go over them with the class.

10. See if your students or parents would like to expand the project. Perhaps a parent would like to organize the planning of a Thanksgiving dinner to be delivered to a needy family. What other ideas does the class have? Perhaps you'd like to involve another class, perhaps the entire school: The sky's the limit on contribution.

LETTER TO PARENTS

Lesson 18
Taking Care of Those Who Are Hungry

Dear Parents,

As Thanksgiving draws near we are reminded of those people who may not be well provided for this year. Our class is collecting canned and dried goods to be given to those in need this Thanksgiving. Could you send in an unopened can or box of non-perishable food for this purpose? Your help will be appreciated by many people.

Do you have any other ideas? If you would like to help us expand our project, please let us know. Thanks for being there.

Much love,

Student's Name

THE BASIC NEEDS OF PEOPLE

OBJECTIVES

- The children will discover that all people have the same basic needs, and that we are all the same inside.

- The children will understand the basic needs we all share: food, clothing, shelter, and love.

- The children will understand that regardless of how people look, act, and live, their basic needs are the same.

MATERIALS

- Chart with the words "Basic Needs of People" hand-lettered on top

- Markers

- *National Geographic* magazines or other magazines and posters with pictures of people from different cultures

- A globe

- Chart paper with the words: "Ways in Which All People Are Alike" hand-lettered on top

PROCEDURE

1. Have the children sit in a circle. Affirm them by reminding them that they are each special and unique. Tell them that everyone on earth has something special about them. Tell them also that we share something with all the people on earth—our basic needs. Have a chart paper hanging in front of the room with the title: "Basic Needs of People." Ask the children to look at the chart.

2. Ask, "What are things or conditions that you need for survival?" (Define survival.) Determine through discussion the differences between needs and wants. Stress that needs are things or conditions we must have in order to live. Wants are optional and do not determine our survival.

3. Have your students state "needs" as you list them on the chart. The basic needs are: food, clothing, shelter, and love. Things connected to these four basics such as medicine, money, etc. can also be included. However, a clear distinction must be made between what people need and want.

4. Show pictures of people from other cultures. Ask, "Do you suppose these people have the same needs as we do?" Discuss. Guide your students to the conclusion that regardless of how differently people look, live, act or speak, they all have the same basic needs. Children can

locate countries on the globe where people in the pictures come from.

5. Focus on the pictures again. Ask, "How are these people different from you? How are they like you?" Ask, "When people look different does that mean their basic needs are different from yours?" Discuss.

6. Focus on pictures of different environmental settings including people in native dress, their homes, families, and foods. Ask, "What basic needs are being met in these pictures?"

7. Say, "Even though people of other cultures may look different from us, in what specific ways are they like us?" List similarities on chart entitled "Ways in Which All People Are Alike."

8. Ask, "If someone does look different, does that mean they are different inside?" Discuss.

9. Tell the children that conflicts are often based on perceived differences (racial, gender, cultural, religious, handicaps). Discuss.

10. Say, "Sometimes differences are perceived as threatening." Explain that sometimes we don't trust people who look and act differently from us. Say, "Sometimes wars have been fought over differences. The important thing to remember is that the basic needs of people are the same no matter how different they appear to be. We are

all interconnected." Define the word "interconnected." Say, "We are the 'human family.' It's important to care about other people, not just about those who are like us. We live on this earth together [indicate wholeness of globe]. We will always be connected as inhabitants of the same planet. Having a peaceful world means accepting each other and knowing we're the same inside, and that we all need the same things. It's also important to remember that all people are special."

11. Ask, "Do you ever find it hard to accept people who seem too different from you?" Discuss.

12. Ask, "Have you ever not been accepted by someone else because they thought you were different?" Discuss.

13. Ask, "If peace starts with you, how do you need to treat others, especially those people who appear to be different?" Discuss. Conclude the lesson with an affirmation of the children. Let them know that they are capable of accepting differences even though it might feel hard for them to do this at times.

WE ARE ALL INTERCONNECTED

OBJECTIVES

- The children will demonstrate the understanding that all people have the same basic needs (food, clothing, shelter, love).

- The children will understand that when people are committed to solving conflicts, they can find ways to resolve them.

- The children will understand that they can change the way they perceive differences by remembering that people all over the world are the same inside and are interconnected (mutually joined or related).

MATERIALS

- Large globe

- A copy of *National Geographic* or other magazine depicting a lifestyle different from our own (e.g., Africa, India, China)

- Piece of clay, string, or yarn

- Yardsticks or long piece of string to use as a "boundary"

- Any photograph depicting war or physical conflict

PROCEDURE

1. Have the children sit in a circle on the floor. Place the globe in the center of the circle.

2. Review the concept that people all over the world need food, clothing, shelter, and love. Show a picture to the children depicting people in a country where the lifestyle is visibly different from their own.

3. Ask the students to look carefully at the picture and to describe how the people are different in the way they live, dress, or look. When appropriate, read descriptive excerpts from the magazine you have chosen. Encourage full participation. Your students may conclude that the houses shown are different because of the climate and the terrain, and that social activities may be different because of the different available facilities. Phrase your questions so the children can begin to hypothesize, draw conclusions, and use creative and critical thinking. Try to get them to draw on their own experience and on facts they may have learned before this lesson, as well as from this new material.

4. Guide your students to consider the similarities between the people in the pictures and people in the United States. Focus on basic

human needs as one commonality we all share, regardless of differences.

5. Guide the children to reiterate that all people have the basic needs of food, clothing, shelter—and love.

6. Using the globe, place a small clay ball as a marker on the country depicted in the picture. Place another on the United States. Connect the two with a small piece of string or yarn. Stress the concept that all people are "interconnected." Define. Ask the children what "interconnected" means to them.

7. Have your students look at the globe. Say, "Astronauts in outer space see the earth as one unit. They also see the earth with no boundaries between nations. In seeing the earth this way, people are reminded that we share one earth; we are all interconnected. Different people in different nations are part of one human family." Explain the meaning of the word "boundaries."

8. Using pictures of battle scenes, discuss how people in different lands have fought over boundaries. Ask the children what sometimes happens when people of one country cross over the boundaries of an enemy country. Discuss.

9.   Have your students play act such a situation. Separate one part of the room from the other with yardsticks or string. Choose children to play the parts of leaders of different countries over which there is a "border" dispute. Ask the class to think of ways the dispute can be settled. Discuss. Repeat the play act using the Win/Win Guidelines.

Stress the fact that sometimes people forget that they're all the same inside, especially during times of disagreement. But the fact remains, people are all the same inside, and that we do have the ability to work out our differences. Say, "Sometimes this seems impossible to us. We get discouraged and feel that we can't settle things peacefully. Sometimes we don't want to settle things peacefully, especially when we're angry. It's the same for our governments.

All those feelings are natural. Just remember, we always have a choice in the way we work out our problems."

10.   Ask, "What generally happens when you hit someone?" The children will probably respond by saying, "They hit me back." Ask, "Then what do you do?" Guide the children to see that one person hitting another usually escalates into a fight. Define the word "escalate." Let the children know that the same thing happens with nations. Say, "When one nation 'hurts' another, and the other nation 'hurts' them back, what can this develop into?" Ask, "How can we prevent this from happening?" Be sure to draw the relationship between individual and global acts. Continue to stress the idea that we always have a choice in the way we act, and choosing hurtful actions usually causes more of the same.

WHAT IS A PEACEMAKER

OBJECTIVES

- The children will understand the qualities of a peacemaker.
- The children will identify times they have been peacemakers.
- The children will understand that peacemaking is not always easy, and that it's important not to give up when we get discouraged.

MATERIALS

- Large chart with the following information: a peacemaker.

A PEACEMAKER IS SOMEONE WHO:

- cares about and accepts others
- cares about and accepts him/herself
- is patient
- helps and affirms others
- is creative and tries to come up with solutions even when there don't seem to be any
- can change his/her mind (is flexible)
- makes positive choices
- has many different feelings, including anger, but tries his or her best to work out conflicts peacefully
- is committed enough to try to work things out even when discouraged
- is forgiving

- A small teacher- or child-made picture of the planet earth

PROCEDURE

1. Ask the children to form a circle. Show the chart "A Peacemaker Is Someone Who." Have the students read the qualities.

2. Ask, "When have you exhibited any of these qualities?" Lead the discussion with your own personal anecdote.

3. Have the children think of a time when they exhibited any of the qualities on the chart. Discuss.

4. Say, "Think about a time when you exhibited one or more of the qualities of a peacemaker." Reread the chart. Say, "Think about yourself as a

peacemaker. Who are you with? What are you doing? What are you saying? How do you feel? Try to recreate that feeling now." Give students a few moments to do this.

5. Say, "We're going to pass the picture of the planet earth around the circle. When you hold it I'd like you to share your experience of being a peacemaker. The picture of the earth reminds us that we are all part of one planet, and that each individual is important."

6. Pass around the picture of the earth. Encourage each child to share a time in which

he or she exhibited at least one quality of a peacemaker. Acknowledge each child warmly, thanking each for participating.

7. Ask, "Is it sometimes hard to be a peacemaker?" Discuss.

8. Share a time when it was hard for you to be a peacemaker.

9. Ask, "Are there times you don't want to be a peacemaker?" Discuss and share a time when you haven't wanted to be a peacemaker yourself.

10. Tell the children that it's human nature to not get along all the time—to be so angry at times that we don't want to make up. State, "The thing to remember is that we always have a choice, and things usually work out better when we choose to be peaceful. That doesn't mean that we have to allow others to be mean or hurtful toward us. What it means is that we try to understand why the other person is acting that way; we try to ask ourselves what else we can do besides being hurtful too."

11. Affirm the children by thanking them for their honesty and willingness to think about these questions.

THINGS I'M GOOD AT

OBJECTIVES

- The children will learn to create a peaceful feeling within.
- The children will identify several different things they are good at.
- The children will draw or write and discuss things they are good at, reinforcing positive self-esteem.

MATERIALS

- Puppet or "I'm Good At" sign (optional)
- Tape recorder and blank tape
- Drawing paper and lined writing paper, crayons

  NOTE: This lesson correlates with Bulletin Board 2, entitled "Things I'm Good At"

PROCEDURE

1. Have the students sit in a circle with legs crossed.

2. Say, "We're going to get very relaxed today before beginning our lesson. We're going to create a peaceful, quiet feeling in our classroom and within ourselves."

3. Say, "Let's take some deep breaths. Breathe slowly and feel the quiet in your bodies." Tell the children that whenever they need to, they can bring back that relaxed feeling by themselves, simply taking slow deep breaths.

4. Now, ask the children to picture themselves doing something they're good at. Suggest different things they like: sports, dance, singing, art, cooking, reading, helping people, figuring out solutions. Younger children can be encouraged to think also about dressing themselves, making their bed, tying their shoelaces, etc.

5. Say, "Now, in your mind, watch yourself doing something you're good at. Most of us are good at many different things, so choose only one for now. How do you look doing the thing you're good at? How do you feel? How do other people feel about you when you're doing this?" Give the children time to think quietly.

6. After a few moments, ask the children to share. Briefly reiterate the Guidelines for Sharing from Lesson 4—no putdowns, etc. Begin the sharing time by telling the children about something you're good at.

7. It's fun to use a puppet with younger children during this lesson; e.g., "Big Bird" might say, "I'm good at helping my friend tie his shoelaces." Pass the puppet around the circle, allowing each child that can use it to say "I'm good at…" With older children, use an "I'm Good At" sign which each child can hold on his or her turn. Tape record the children speaking.

8. After each child has had a turn, have the class return to their seats and draw and/or write about themselves doing the thing they're good at. For young children, the teacher can write: "[name] is good at [activity]" on top of each child's paper. Older children can do this independently. Play back the tape while the children draw and write.

9. To conclude the lesson, have the children share their pictures and/or stories with one another in small groups and discuss.

Bulletin Board 2
Learning the Skills of Peacemaking

Children's drawings

Children's names

THINGS I'M GOOD AT!

USING PEACEMAKING LOGS

OBJECTIVES

- The children will learn more about the process of keeping a Peacemaking Log.

- The children will understand the purpose of their Peacemaking Log.

- The children will draw and write their idea of a peaceful classroom.

MATERIALS

- Children's logs—black and white composition notebooks for older children. Notebooks with blank paper for younger children

- Teacher's Log (keeping your own Peacemaking Log is an essential part of the process)

- Peacemaking Log Box—a large cardboard box, covered to your taste and labeled

PROCEDURE

1. Prior to this lesson, make sure each child has brought in the notebook which will serve as his/her Peacemaking Log throughout the year. Tell the class that you will be discussing many new ideas this year, and that the log will serve three purposes:

- It will be a place where each child can express his/her thoughts and feelings on specific topics

- It will be a place where each child can express thoughts whenever they come up in all areas of peacemaking

- It will be a place in which to discover solutions to problems through writing or drawing

2. Show your log to the class. Explain that you will be writing along with them, and from time to time you will read your log entries to the class. Explain that the process of peacemaking is something new and that you will all be learning about it together. Say, "You will also learn about yourselves through the process of keeping a log."

3. Ask the children if any of them ever has kept any kind of log before. Ask if they know the purpose of log-keeping (self-knowledge). Discuss. Tell your class that the more people learn about themselves, the better they relate to the people around them. State: "Having a

world at peace means relating well to ourselves and others. Writing in a log helps this happen."

4. Tell your class, "The most important thing in this kind of writing is to freely express your ideas without judging them. Whatever you write will be fine. Spelling, neatness, and grammar don't count. The only thing that matters is letting your ideas flow." Discuss. Some children may be concerned that they won't have any ideas, or that their ideas won't be good enough. Allow them to express their concerns, and assure them that there is no right or wrong way to express oneself in log-writing. Say, "Our minds are filled with thoughts, ideas, and feelings. The log is the place where we can bring all of this out of our minds and onto paper."

5. Show your class the Peacemaking Log Box. Tell them that they will put their logs in this box after each entry, and then the logs will be returned to them. Say, "If you want to express ideas, thoughts, or feelings at any time, you can write in your log and place it in the box for me to read. If you don't want me to read something, put a paper clip on that page and I will be sure not to look at it."

6. State, "Now we're going to do our first log entry. The topic is 'My Idea of a Peaceful Classroom.' "

7. State, "Take some slow, deep breaths and think of our classroom being empty. This is the beginning of a new day. It's bright and sunny, and you feel wonderful. Now fill the room with children, and have them treating each other in a way that makes everyone feel accepted and at home. Think of all the children being together in this way. What does it feel like? How do you feel? What are you learning about in this classroom? What do you most want to learn about? How do you feel coming to school in this kind of classroom?" Have the children think of their ideas quietly for a few moments.

8. State, "Now write down what you just pictured." Drawing is appropriate for young children. "Describe what you saw, how you felt, what the other people were doing. Anything you write or draw is fine."

9. Give the class five to ten minutes to work. Older children can draw in their logs, also. Say, "If you have an idea in your mind to go along with what you are writing, draw it on the opposite page."

10. Ask the class if anyone would like to share their log entries with the class. Let them know that they don't ever have to share their log entries. Remind your students that there are no put-downs or negative comments of any kind about other people's log entries. Say, "Peace begins within each of us. Accepting others and what others have to say is a big part of this."

11. Discuss the log entries together. Have the children place their logs in the box each time they have made an entry. Return them with your responses when appropriate.

PEACEMAKING LOGS: FEELING SPECIAL

OBJECTIVES

- The children will engage in the process of keeping a Peacemaking Log.
- The children will recall a time they felt special, thereby building self-esteem.

MATERIALS

- Teacher's Peacemaking Log
- Logs, pencils, pens, crayons
- Peacemaking Log Box

PROCEDURE

1. Have the children sit in a circle. Say, "You had your first experience in log writing during our last lesson. Is there anyone who didn't read his or her last log entry aloud last time who would like to do so now? This is entirely optional." Young children can describe and show their drawings.

2. Tell the children that no judgements or criticisms are to be made on anyone's entries. Allow time for brief discussion.

3. Say, "Today we're going to focus on something new in our logs."

4. Say, "Remember, a log usually describes someone's feelings, thoughts, or responses. The best logs are those in which the writer expresses his/her feelings freely. When you write in your log, allow your feelings to flow out of you, and write them down exactly the way they are. Also remember spelling, grammar, and neatness are not important when we write in our logs. The most important thing is that you express your ideas."

5. State, "Each of you is a special and unique individual. You are an important part of the world in which we live. Each of you has the ability to make a huge difference in the world, and your thoughts are very important. Respect your own thoughts. They are a special part of you."

6. Say, "Now we're going to do an exercise in which we will recall a time we felt special or important."

7. Say, "Let's get very relaxed. Let your body become very still and quiet. Take some deep breaths and listen to the calmness in the room. Take another deep breath in through your nose and out through your nose. Now recall the smell of a flower. Breathe in deeply and smell the fragrance. Let the fragrance go deep inside of you. Breathe in again and allow the beautiful fragrance of the flower to move throughout your entire body. Now just let your body relax and imagine that the whole room is filled with the fragrance of your flower."

8. State, "I'm going to ask you to recall a time when you felt special or important. It can be a time when you may have helped another person, or a time when you were given a new responsibility, a time when you learned to do something new, or any other time when you felt special. Picture yourself doing whatever you were doing at the time. How did you feel? How did you look? Picture the expression on your face, the position of your body. Recall the thoughts you had about yourself when you were feeling so special. Recapture that feeling again now." Give the children one to two minutes to think about this.

9. State, "How do you feel?" Allow children to share.

10. Ask, "Who would like to share about the time you just recalled, a time of feeling special and important?" Allow the children time to share. You can share first.

11. Ask, "Is there anyone who had difficulty recalling a time of feeling special or important?" If anyone says yes, offer to speak to that child privately at a later time if he/she wishes. Do a little "coaching," and see if you can help to bring about some positive recollection.

12. State, "Now we're going to write in our logs what we just recalled. [Younger children will draw.] Be descriptive. Write [draw] about your feelings, the situation, how you reacted and what it was like. Allow the feelings to guide your pen [crayon]. Don't be afraid of making mistakes." If there are one or two who can't recall a time of feeling special or important, now is the time to speak with them privately.

13. Allow students about ten minutes in which to write or draw. Children who write and finish early can draw a picture to go along with their entry, start a new entry on a topic they choose, or read a book.

14. Ask the children to place their logs in the box at the end of the lesson.

15. Log entries can be discussed the following day.

PEACEMAKER OF THE WEEK

OBJECTIVES

- The students who have applied the Win/Win Guidelines and who have exhibited the qualities of a peacemaker will receive recognition for their efforts and actions.

- The students will evaluate their own and each others' actions according to how well they exemplify peacemaking behavior.

MATERIALS

- Peacemakers of the Week Award Certificate (Page 113)

- Win/Win Guidelines poster from Lesson 10 for review

- "A Peacemaker Is Someone Who" chart from Lesson 21 for review

- A 5" x 8" file box or any similar box for peacemaker nominations, labeled "Peacemaker of the Week"

- Notecards

   NOTE: This lesson corresponds with the "Peacemakers of the Week" bulletin board at the end of this lesson.

PROCEDURE

1. Have the class sit in a circle on the floor.

2. Say, "I'd like you to take some deep breaths and find a peaceful place inside. In that place, think about the way you treated people this week. Think about your friends in school, your family, people on your block, or people you don't know that well. Think about a time this week when you acted like a peacemaker. You may have used the Win/Win Guidelines to work out a problem, you may have affirmed someone, or you may have helped another person. In your mind, look at the other person's face and see how he/she feels. Now feel your own feelings. Think about this, and in a moment I'm going to ask you to share your experiences."

3. Go around the circle giving each child a chance to respond to the statement, "I was a peacemaker when…"

4. After sharing, affirm the class. Example: "I want to acknowledge you all for living the words 'Peace begins with me.' Being a peacemaker takes effort and concern. I know you will each make a difference in the world as the result of your efforts."

5. Say, "To recognize how important your efforts as peacemakers are, we are going to start a special program called, 'Peacemakers of the Week.' Each week we will pick two students as the Peacemakers of the Week. One

will be nominated by the students and one will be selected by the teacher. Each will receive this award certificate." (Show sample certificate.) This also can be done with only one student each week.

6.   Have a class discussion to devise guidelines for selecting a person for the Peacemaker of the Week Award. Brainstorm as a group the ways a person should act to be selected. Refer to the poster for Win/Win Guidelines and "A Peacemaker Is Someone Who..."

7.   Say, "On a notecard, write your name, the date, and the name of someone you feel is a peacemaker in our class. Describe specifically how that person acted as a peacemaker." Do a sample one on the board. Example: "Tommy was a peacemaker when he helped me with my math." Say, "Put the nomination notecard in the Peacemaker of the Week Box. We will use the nominations to select our Peacemakers of the Week."

8.   The process you may want to use for student selection is to list on the board the nominations in the box, then have others speak on behalf of the nominations. The selection could then be by private ballot.

9.   The teacher can select the second Peacemaker of the Week based on observations of the children throughout the week.

10. End the lesson by selecting two Peacemakers of the Week and awarding them each a certificate.

11. Follow up: Ask students each day if they are thinking of how they and others are acting as peacemakers and whom they will nominate. Do the awarding the same day each week or on alternating weeks so students can look forward to it. You can provide extra recognition for recipients by asking them to bring a photo of themselves to school to be placed on a "Peacemakers of the Week" bulletin board. You can also keep a "Peacemaker Honor Roll," a permanent list to be hung on this bulletin board, on which each "Peacemaker of the Week" appears.

> NOTE: Some teachers have several peacemakers each week or alternating week. It's a good idea to give some extra coaching to children who aren't as apt to receive this award. Help them discover specific things they can do to be regarded as a peacemaker, so they can win the award too. I usually make sure every child wins the award once before anyone wins it twice.

Bulletin Board 3

Learning the Skills of Peacemaking

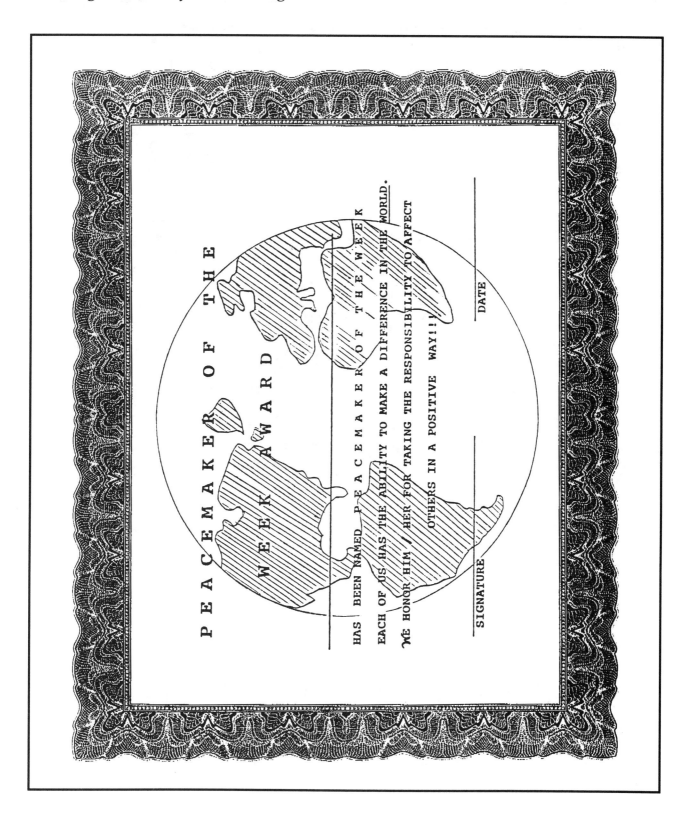

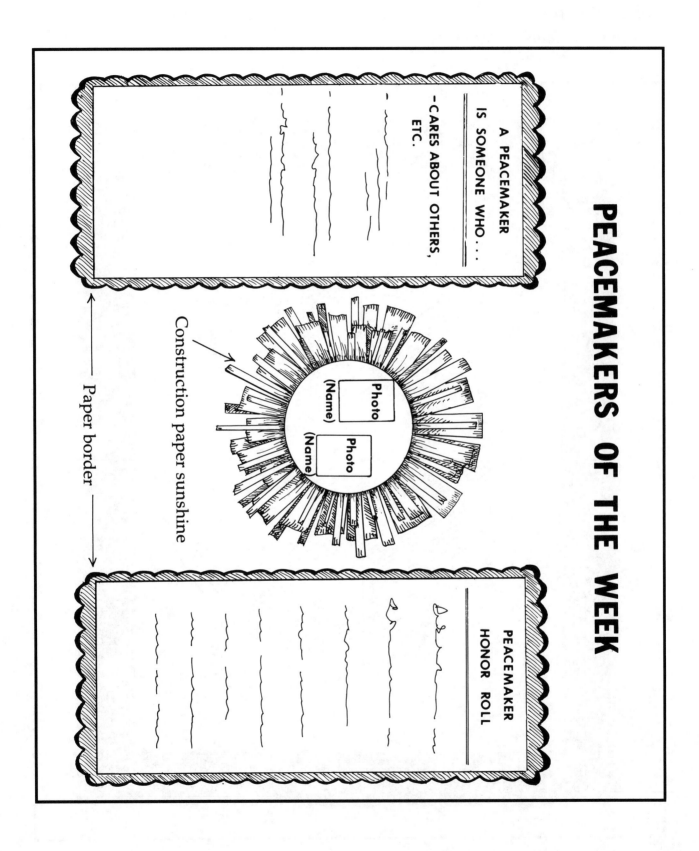

PEACEMAKERS OF THE WEEK

A PEACEMAKER IS SOMEONE WHO . . . .

—CARES ABOUT OTHERS, ETC.

Paper border

Construction paper sunshine

Photo
(Name)

Photo
(Name)

PEACEMAKER HONOR ROLL

PEACEMAKERS IN MY LIFE

OBJECTIVES

- The children will review the qualities of a peacemaker.
- The children will identify and describe people they know who exhibit these qualities.
- The children will identify people they've heard about who are peacemakers.

MATERIALS

- A selected story or article about a peacemaker (Martin Luther King, Gandhi, Rosa Parks, etc.) See resource section for suggested books.
- "A Peacemaker Is Someone Who..." chart from Lesson 21
- Logs, pencils, crayons

PROCEDURE

1. Have children sit in a circle. Read the story or article describing the peacemaker you have chosen.

2. Refer to the "A Peacemaker Is Someone Who..." chart. Ask, "What qualities did this person exhibit?" Discuss.

3. Ask, "What do you admire most about this person?" Discuss.

4. Ask, "How would our world be different if there were more people like _____?" Discuss.

5. Say, "Now I'd like you to take a few moments and think about people in your life who are peacemakers. They should be ordinary people—not famous people in the news. Remember, all people who ended up becoming famous peacemakers started off as ordinary people, just like us."

6. Have each child turn to the person he/she is sitting next to. Ask each child to share with his/her partner about the peacemaker they are thinking of.

7. After about four minutes, have the children face forward in the circle. Ask them to describe the peacemaker in their lives, and to tell what qualities they exhibit which make them peacemakers.

8. Say, "Do you think it's ever hard for these people to be peacemakers?" Discuss. Ask, "Do you think they ever get angry and act in ways that aren't peaceful?" Discuss. Ask, "Do you think it's possible to be a peacemaker even if there are times you are not peaceful?" Discuss. Say, "One quality that helps people to be peacemakers is commitment. When you are committed to something, that doesn't mean you never make mistakes. It means you keep trying even after you have made a mistake." Give a personal example.

9. Using the Peacemaking Logs, ask the children to draw and/or write a picture and/or story about an ordinary person in their lives whom they think is a peacemaker.

10. Have the children share their stories and pictures and discuss them.

MEASURING THE UNDERSTANDINGS LEARNED IN THIS GUIDE

STAGE I: Peace Begins With Me

NOTE: This page can be used in two different ways. For younger children you can ask the questions aloud as a means of review. This will enable you to find out how much of the content they are absorbing. For older children you can use this page as an informal test to measure the depth of understanding of concepts.

1. What does peace mean to you?

2. What are the qualities of a peacemaker?

3. Which of these qualities have you shown in your own life?

4. What are the Win/Win Guidelines used for?

5. List the Win/Win Guidelines in your own words.

6. How have you applied the Win/Win Guidelines in your life?

7. What is an "I Message"? Give two examples.

8. What does it mean to affirm someone? Give an example.

9. What are the basic needs of people?

10. How can the world be a better place through the use of peacemaking skills?

STAGE II: INTEGRATING PEACEMAKING INTO OUR LIVES

If there is right in the soul,
There will be beauty in the person;

If there is beauty in the person,
There will be harmony in the home;

If there is harmony in the home,
There will be order in the nation;
If there is order in the nation,
There will be peace in the world.

LAO TZU

PEACE STARTS WITH ME

OBJECTIVES

- The children will develop another dimension of understanding how peace starts with the individual.

- The children will develop an understanding that there are different ways people experience peace as individuals.

- The children will develop an understanding that if people want a peaceful home, school, community, world, then it is up to each individual to take responsibility for his/her own interactions.

MATERIALS

- Poster:

> WE TAKE CARE OF OUR BODIES BY:
>
> Observing safety rules
>
> Getting proper rest and sleep
>
> Eating healthy foods
>
> Getting proper dental care
>
> Having regular check-ups at the doctor

- Poster:

> WE KEEP OUR MINDS HEALTHY BY:
>
> Learning and going to school
>
> Giving ourselves time to rest and relax
>
> Having someone to talk to when we have a problem (Mom, Dad, friends)
>
> Knowing how to relax when we are under stress
>
> > (Stress is the nervous, unsettled feeling we get when we're afraid or pressured)

- Drawing paper (for "When I Feel Peaceful, I Look Like This")
- Crayons or markers
- Peacemaking Logs

PROCEDURE

1. Say, "Let's form our circle. We're going to start off with some deep breathing."

2. After a minute or so ask if this helps the children to feel calm and peaceful. Let them know they can can take this feeling everywhere they go.

3. Ask: "What does it feel like to be calm inside?" Have the children share. Focus on the quiet, relaxed feelings that they describe. Discuss these feelings. Have the children give specific descriptions of their calm, peaceful feelings. (For example: "My body feels warm and still," or "I feel happy inside.")

4. State, "Think of other times you have felt this way. Can you describe them?" Children share their recollections.

5. State, "There are different ways we can feel peaceful inside. As you've described, sometimes pleasant circumstances and events can bring forth that feeling within us. Sometimes we feel that way when we're with special people. In all cases, where do peaceful feelings start?" Guide children to the understanding that peacefulness begins within each individual.

6. Say, "People also tend to feel peaceful when they take care of their well-being." Remind the class that well-being is the state you're in when your mind and body feel healthy and taken care of. Ask, "What are some ways we take care of our bodies?" Refer to the "We Take Care of Our Bodies" poster. Other examples can be added from the children's experiences.

7. Ask, "When our minds are strong and healthy, we have good mental health. How do we take care of our minds?" Responses can be listed on the "We Keep Our Minds Healthy" poster. Ask, "What do you do to relax?" Have the children add to the list.

8. Ask, "When you feel peaceful inside, how do you usually act with others?" Discuss. "When you feel stressful, tense, or frightened, how do you act with others?" Discuss. "Think of a time when your body wasn't at peace, like when you were hurt, or very hungry, or very tired. Did you act any differently with the people around you?"

9. State, "There are three main things to remember about being peaceful inside: (1) We are all responsible for our well-being. We must take proper care of our minds and bodies. (2) When we don't take care of ourselves—for example, if we stay up too late or don't eat properly—we tend not to feel and act peacefully. (3) We always have a choice in the way we act. Even when we don't feel peaceful, a peaceful place still lives inside us. We can choose to act from that place, and to do the things necessary for our health and well-being."

10. State, "Remember how quiet and peaceful you felt after breathing deeply. Remember other times you felt that way inside. Try to bring that feeling back again. Find the place inside you where that feeling lives. Recreate the peaceful feeling." Children do this for one to two minutes.

11. Ask, "Were you able to bring the feeling back?" Discuss briefly. Stress the fact that all people have the ability to find the peaceful place within. If you practice doing this every day, it will become easier. This exercise can help anyone in the class whenever you feel upset, nervous, or frightened."

12. Ask, "If we want a peaceful home, school, community, world, with whom does it begin?" State, "Remember, taking care of ourselves helps us be peaceful. Also, we always have a choice in the way we act with others. As human beings we have the ability to choose peaceful actions, and if we make a mistake, there's always next time. We all make mistakes, and sometimes we disappoint ourselves and others. That doesn't mean there's anything wrong with us. You're still a special person, you've just made a mistake, that's all."

13. Pass out drawing paper. Have children draw pictures and title them, "When I Feel Peaceful I Look Like This." Pictures should also include the people and activities related to the feeling of peacefulness.

14. Allow the children to share and discuss their pictures.

15. Older children can do a related written log entry. Younger children can continue in their log by drawing another peaceful situation.

MAKING ETHICAL CHOICES I

OBJECTIVES

- The children will examine several ethical dilemmas.

- The children will learn the meaning of the term "morals."

- The children will make decisions about how to handle a situation in which a choice has to be made between right and wrong.

- The children will learn the meaning of the term "morals."

MATERIALS

- Peacemaking Logs
- Pencils

PROCEDURE

1. Have the children sit in a circle. Say, "Have you ever been in a situation where you had to make a decision between right and wrong?" Discuss briefly.

2. Tell about a situation you have been in where you were faced with an ethical dilemma. Discuss.

3. Share the following ethical dilemma that I was in:

When my boys were 11 and 8, we went out of our area to try a new shopping center. We went into a women's clothing store where I tried on an evening dress with a $100 necklace. Deciding against the purchase, I changed and we went back to the car to proceed home. When we got half-way home, I realized I was still wearing the necklace. My thought was, "I don't have time to turn around and go back to the store now. I'll return it tomorrow."

When I told my boys that I was still wearing the necklace, Michael adamantly said, "You have to turn around right now and return that necklace. It wouldn't be right to wait." He was shocked that I'd even consider it.

"Mom," said Tim, "did you think about keeping the necklace?"

"You know, Tim," I said, "It crossed my mind for about a split second, but I knew it wouldn't be right to do that."

"Why?" he asked. "You wouldn't have gotten caught, and you wouldn't be hurting anyone."

"It would have been wrong," I said. "It wasn't mine to keep. Also, what kind of example would I have been setting for you boys? Now let's hurry up and get back to that store before it closes."

4. Ask your children their reactions to this story. Ask how many thought I should have kept the necklace. Why?

Ask what might have been the consequences of that action.

5. Bring up the term "morals" (making the distinction between right and wrong). Ask why it is important for people to have morals. Discuss.

Ask, "What would the world be like if no one had morals to guide them?" Discuss.

6. Have the class reflect on the following scenario:

> Pete and Jamal are playing baseball. Pete hits a fly ball which crashes through the window of a nearby house. Nobody is at home. What should the boys do?

Discuss. Then have the children write in their logs about the choice they would make and why.

MAKING ETHICAL CHOICES II

OBJECTIVES

• The children will learn the meaning of "integrity."

• The children will reflect upon situations where they'll need to choose between right and wrong.

• The children will work in cooperative groups to come up with a joint decision about an ethical issue.

MATERIALS

• Peacemaking Logs

• Overhead projector

• Transparencies with questions listed in steps 5 and 9 of this lesson (See Appendix)

• Paper and pencil for each group

• Notepaper and clipboard for the teacher

PROCEDURE

1. Have the children form a circle. Go over the terms "morals" and "consequences." Introduce the term "integrity" (being of sound moral principle; honest). Ask the children if any of these words have a personal meaning in their lives. Discuss.

2. Ask what other thoughts the children may have had about the concept of morals or moral behavior since the last lesson. Ask if anyone wants to share their log entry from the last lesson. Discuss.

3. Say, "We're going to get into cooperative groups with four people in each group. You'll be working together to decide how to handle several different situations where moral issues are at stake. I want you to think of the kind of decisions you would actually make if you were in these situations. Be honest with yourselves and the people in your group. Don't pick an answer because you think it's the one I want to hear." Make sure everyone is clear on this.

   NOTE: Before beginning, assign roles to each member of your cooperative groups. You'll need:

• a leader to facilitate the group.

• a recorder to take notes on any decisions the group makes, and to report the decisions back to the class.

• two affirmers who will acknowledge and thank each person who shares. They will also encourage those who are quiet to participate.

4. Have your class get into groups and assign roles. Carefully explain and model each role before having the children begin. Remind the children that the way they work together should exemplify their knowledge of peacemaking.

5. Show the following scenario on a transparency:

> Mr. Ruiz is giving a spelling test to the class. Karen didn't have time to study last night. The words are really hard. She doesn't want to fail the test. When Mr. Ruiz looks away, Karen realizes she can clearly see the answers on Carlita's paper. Carlita always gets A's.
>
> What should Karen do?

6. Give each group 5-10 minutes to discuss the question. Circulate among the groups and make sure they're staying on track and speaking from the heart. You can make notations to share with them later as to how each group functioned.

7. Have the groups get back into a circle. Ask each recorder to share what decisions were made in their group and why. Ask for opposing viewpoints. It's important that diverse feelings

be aired so you can address them and offer guidance.

8.   As each group shares give input on how the group worked together. Also bring up the term "integrity." See if the children understand how it relates to the scenario they just discussed.

9.   Go on to the next scenario:

Sean, Patrick, and their parents are visiting Mr. and Mrs. Gold and 2-year-old Simon. Mr. and Mrs. Gold ask Sean and Patrick to take Simon into the den and play with him. They all start rough-housing and Patrick falls into an expensive lamp, breaking it. Mr. Gold comes running into the room, saying, "Is everything okay?" Patrick says, "Nobody's hurt but Simon got a little wild and ran into this lamp." He points to the broken remains. "We're sorry he did that but we couldn't stop him in time." Sean is upset, knowing Patrick is lying.

What should Sean do?

10. Have the class get back into cooperative groups and follow the same procedure as before.

11. Conclude by having the class reflect on the discussions that just took place. Ask them to write in their Peacemaking Logs about how they would have handled these two situations.

MAKING ETHICAL CHOICES III

OBJECTIVES

- The children will show understanding of the meanings of morals, integrity, and consequences.

- The children will look at moral issues of a more serious nature and make decisions as to how they should be handled.

- The children will work in cooperative groups to make decisions.

- The children will reflect on moral issues in their logs.

MATERIALS

- Peacemaking Logs
- Transparency with scenario outlined in step 5 (See Appendix)
- Overhead projector
- Paper and pencil for each group
- Teacher's notepaper and clipboard

PROCEDURE

1. Have the class form a circle. Ask the children what thoughts they've had about the issue of integrity since the last lesson. See if anyone wants to share their log entries from that lesson. Discuss.

2. Ask, "What does it mean to have high morals?" Discuss. Ask, "What kinds of consequences are there for not being guided by morals?" Discuss both inner and outer consequences.

3. Ask, "What kinds of problems would we have in our community if people were never guided by integrity and morals?" Discuss.

4. Tell the children they'll be working in cooperative groups again to look at some more issues that kids are sometimes faced with. Let them know they'll be keeping the same roles as last time.

> NOTE: When working with cooperative groups it's best to let the children keep the same roles for several weeks before rotating. This way they can get comfortable with the roles they are doing. By the way, this technique adapts well to all content areas.

5. Show the following scenario:

Mark and Nayeem are on the playground. It's Saturday and no one else is around. Mark says, "Look what I have, Nayeem," as he pulls out two cigarettes. "Where'd you get those?" asks Nayeem. "You know cigarettes aren't good for you."

"Don't be a baby," says Mark, laughing. "I took these out of my mom's dresser when she went to work. She'll never know they're missing. Besides, it's cool to smoke. My mom does and so does my brother. Here, have one."

What should Nayeem do?

---

6. Follow the same procedure as in the last two lessons. Children work in cooperative groups to address the question. Teacher circulates. Then the class gets back into a circle to share and debrief. Make sure you bring up the issues of integrity and consequences in the class discussion.

7. In their logs, have the children reflect on what was discussed. Ask them to write about how they would have handled the situation if they were Nayeem. Have them also write about the consequences of going along with Mark.

MAKING ETHICAL CHOICES IV

OBJECTIVES

- The children will show understanding of the terms integrity, morals, and consequences.

- The children will examine a more difficult moral issue than in previous lessons. They will make decisions as to how it should be handled.

- The children will work in cooperative groups to come up with a decision.

- The children will write in logs about how they would handle a difficult moral dilemma.

MATERIALS

- Peacemaking Logs

- Overhead projector

- Transparency with scenario for step 4 of this lesson (See Appendix)

- Paper and pencil for each group

- Notepaper and clipboard for the teacher

PROCEDURE

1. Have the children sit in a circle. Ask them to share log responses from the last lesson (voluntary, as with all log sharing). Have them respond to one another's log entries.

2. Address the issues of integrity and consequences as related to this discussion. By now the children should be showing a real understanding of these two concepts.

3. Ask the class if these discussions have been helpful. How? Ask them what they've learned from these discussions.

4. Have the class get into cooperative groups once more. Show the following scenario:

> Tony's invited to Josh's house after school today. Josh is one of the "cool" kids. Tony's never been invited to one of their get-togethers before. There's a big noisy group of kids all over the house. Josh's parents aren't home from work yet. When Tony goes into the kitchen, he notices several of the kids drinking liquor straight from a bottle they have gotten out of the cabinet above the refrigerator. Tony watches and asks, "What about Josh's parents?"

> "It's cool, man," says Linda. "Josh's parents are gonna be late. There's no way we can get caught." She offers the bottle to Tony. He hesitates and looks a little nervous.

> One of the other kids says, "Don't be a nerd, man. Have some." Tony doesn't know what to do. He knows he's only in sixth grade and he knows drinking's wrong, but he wants the other kids to like him.

> What should Tony do?

5. Follow the same format as in previous lessons. Have the children get into their cooperative groups and address this issue as you circulate.

6. Have the class get back into a large circle and discuss the decisions and insights that arose in their groups. Bring in the issues of integrity and consequences.

7. Have the class write in their logs about how they would have handled this situation and why.

Make time to get the class back together later this week to share log entries, afterthoughts, and insights.

CONNECTING TO THE WORLD AROUND US

NOTE: The Current Events Letter to Parents (page 136) should be discussed in class and sent home prior to this lesson.

OBJECTIVES

- The children will evaluate a current events article dealing with either peace or the environment. Younger children can use articles from *Scholastic News* or *Weekly Reader*.

- The children will draw their own conclusions based on information in the article.

- The children will brainstorm solutions to problems in the article.

- The children will work collaboratively to attempt to reach an agreement.

     NOTE: Younger children will need one aide or helper per brainstorming group.

MATERIALS

- Large poster entitled "Ways We Become Well-Informed"

- A selected current events article (for the teacher)

- Children's articles

- One large chart-size paper per group of five children

- One magic marker per group

PROCEDURE

1. Have the students form a circle and bring their articles. Say, "Remember the word 'contribution'? What does that mean?" Focus on the meaning of contribution as a way people can give of themselves to those around them, or to society in general.

2. Say, "Can you think of anyone who makes a contribution to the world around us?" Briefly discuss.

3. Say, "One of the ways we can all make a contribution is by being well-informed." Explain the meaning of the word "well-informed." Say, "As citizens of our country and of the world, we can stay informed in many different ways. What are some of the ways we stay informed?" List the students' ideas on the "Ways We Become Well-Informed" chart. Examples can be: read the newspapers, listen to the radio, watch the news, have class and family discussions, go places.

4. Say, "You have all become better informed by learning about the news in your articles." Have each student briefly tell the person he or she is sitting next to about his/her article.

5. Say, "Today we're going to inform ourselves about..." [main idea of article you have chosen]. "I am going to read you an article I brought in that we will discuss together. After I read it, I'd like you to come up with solutions to the problem addressed in this article."

6. Read the article to the class.

7. Define terms used in the article. It is best to give some background before doing this. Also, articles with pictures engage the children more. With younger children you might have to paraphrase the entire article.

8. Discuss the article.

9. Ask, "What problem is focused on?"

10. Divide the children into "problem-solving groups" of four or five. Tell the students that they will discuss solutions in their groups.

11. Ask the students in each group to choose a leader. Tell the students they must decide on their leader quietly, calmly, peacefully, and quickly. Let them decide how to choose. For young children, the aide or helper will assist at this point.

12. Then ask the students to come up with solutions. Ask, "How can we deal with this problem in a way that satisfies the needs of all involved?"

13. Give the students seven to ten minutes to brainstorm ideas, record, and discuss. Circulate and coach.

14. After the allotted time, ask each group to choose one solution to the problem.

15. Give a few more minutes. Tell the students that the agreement must be reached calmly and fairly, so no one loses. Remind them of the Win/Win Guidelines if conflicts arise.

16. After five minutes, see how many groups actually came to an agreement. Ask the group leaders to report on how the agreement was reached, or what caused any lack of agreement.

17. Discuss the dynamics of group interaction and the feelings of the participants.

18. Guide the students to the understanding that agreements in groups are not always easy to reach—especially with critical issues. Stress that being a good citizen of the world means working hard and creating solutions even in the face of difficulties. Also stress that there are no easy answers—it is up to all of us to create the solutions.

NOTE: Some students may become very engaged in the problems focused on in the article. Encourage them to write "Letters to the Editor," or to other people related to the issue, expressing their views. Mail all letters.

SAMPLE LETTER
Learning the Skills of Peacemaking
Lesson 32

Dear Friends,

Let's all try to make peace in the world. Let's try not to fight. We need peace in the world to live. We do not like wars. Wars make lots of people die. We don't want you to die either. We should make friends with each other. We should be nice to all other people. We should love each other. When you fight with your brother and sister, please make friends.

Please do not fight to live — make peace. We hope we can all be friends.

People are nice everywhere!

Love,

The Boys & Girls of Mrs. Drew's Class

This letter was subsequently sent to a teacher in Russia. The children also expressed their concerns in letters to the local newspapers. The exercise was a powerful example of the fact that we can all make a difference regardless of our ages.

NOTE: This lesson can be done repeatedly throughout the year, focusing on different issues.

CURRENT EVENTS LETTER TO PARENTS
Learning the Skills of Peacemaking
Lesson 32

Dear Parents,

Throughout the year our class will be doing current events lessons based on things the children are learning in *Learning the Skills of Peacemaking*. You can help enormously by doing the following:

a. Provide your child with a newspaper or magazine to look through (younger children can take a look at a recent issue of *Scholastic News* and locate an article within it).

b. Ask your child what kind of article is needed.

c. Assist your child in locating the particular article, if necessary.

d. Make certain the article is appropriate for your child, not frightening or too complex.

e. Read the article with your child and help him or her summarize it orally.

f. Explain unfamiliar terms or ideas.

Today, your child needs a current events article on _____.
Thanks so much for your help.

Sincerely,

(Teacher's name)

OUR VISIONS ARE SPECIAL

OBJECTIVES

- The children will identify their personal dreams or beliefs in life.
- The children will think about and then draw or write their belief.

    NOTE: This lesson correlates with Bulletin Board 4 entitled "Our Beliefs are Special."

MATERIALS

- Poster:

> "The first thing about winning is to believe you can do it; after that it takes hard work, determination, and support of others."
>
> Wilma Rudolph

- "The Dream of Winning"—Wilma Rudolph (see page 138)
- Cloud patterns, cotton, paste, 9" x 12" white paper, and crayons, or large white paper for freehand drawings
- Tape recorder and blank tape
- Books from the library on Wilma Rudolph (optional)
- Logs, pencils, crayons

PROCEDURE

1. Have the children form a circle and take some deep breaths.

2. Say, "Today we're going to talk about our personal beliefs." Explain that you will focus on a special goal each person has of something he or she wants to achieve in life.

3. Read the quote by Wilma Rudolph on winning. Explain that Wilma Rudolph had a dream of winning a race, and that dream began when she was unable to walk. Explain that winning doesn't necessarily mean beating someone else. People can win at life without having to defeat anyone.

4. Read "The Dream of Winning" (see page 138). Discuss.

5. Ask the students what dreams or ideas they have had for themselves. Tell them it's fine to have whatever positive beliefs they want, that

nothing is too unrealistic to want to achieve. Say, "When Wilma Rudolph created her vision of running a race and winning, she couldn't even walk. It was her dream that gave her the strength and hope to move forward. What is your personal belief?"

6. Have the children think about their beliefs. Keep reiterating that no idea is too outrageous. Say, "Some of the most wonderful inventions and achievements in the world emerged from outrageous ideas."

7. Give the students several minutes to "think." Guide the children by asking: "What are you doing in your belief? How are you dressed? Are you with people or alone? How does it feel to be in your belief right now?"

8. Have students take turns sharing by going around the circle. Tape record each child. Affirm each belief by thanking every child who shares.

9. Pass out cloud patterns (on page 139) for reproduction and paper, or blank paper for freehand drawing. Have the students create their beliefs in the cloud. When completed the children can paste cotton around the edges. Play back the tape.

10. Put the "Our Beliefs are Special" pictures on the bulletin board.

11. Have the children discuss their beliefs in small groups.

12. The children can do a log entry: "My Personal Belief." Older children can write about their beliefs. Younger children can draw, this time about a different belief than what was expressed on the cloud.

THE DREAM OF WINNING

Wilma Rudolph (1940-1994)*

Can you imagine what it would be like to lose your ability to walk? That's what happened to champion Wilma Rudolph when she was 4 years old. She got pneumonia, scarlet fever and then polio at the same time. She was very sick. She nearly died. Her left leg became so weak that she couldn't walk. Not Wilma. Even though she was forced to sit in a chair, she still tried to play games with all her friends. Wilma had hope, and that kept her going. She was determined that one day, somehow, she would walk again.

Fortunately for Wilma, her family loved her very much. Both her parents worked full-time with only one day off each week. On that day Wilma's mother would drive her to the doctor in Nashville, Tennessee, 45 miles away. The doctor would massage Wilma's leg, to make it grow stronger.

Wilma had 22 brothers and sisters! Her mother taught 3 of them how to massage Wilma's leg. They massaged it 4 times a day.

Very slowly Wilma became stronger. When she was 6, she got a pair of special shoes. She could stand up and hop around on one leg. Finally, at the age of 11, Wilma was able to walk and run on her own, without any special shoes. Her hope had gotten her through!

Once she was able to move on her own, Wilma just couldn't be stopped. She started playing basketball. She soon made the school team. She was tall and thin. She could race down the court and shoot baskets better than anyone else. In her sophomore year, she scored 803 points in 25 games! It was an astonishing feat.

Wilma was even more astonishing when she took to track. She had a way of running that was pure poetry. Someone described it as "loose and sweet." Her body seemed to flow. Her arms pumped in rhythm. She seemed to fun faster than any woman alive.

Wilma wanted to prove she was the best. At the age of 16 she entered the Olympics. Her relay team won a third place bronze medal. But when she ran by herself in the 200-meter dash, she didn't do well at all.

Wilma spent the next 4 years training. Every day she forced herself to run and run and then run some more.

When the 1960 Olympics arrived, Wilma was ready. She entered all the track events. She ended up winning 3 gold medals, a new record! Her team took first place in the 400-meter relay. By herself, she won the 100-meter dash and the 200-meter dash.

The world fell in love with Wilma. In Russia, people called her "Queen of the Olympics." In France, she was called "The Gazelle." And in Italy, they named her "The Black Pearl."

Just 16 years before, the fastest woman on earth had been unable to walk. The world will never forget the triumph on Wilma Rudolph. Today Wilma Rudolph is head of the Wilma Rudolph Foundation. The purpose of the foundation is to help young people dream and achieve in the field of sports competition, as well as build character and self-image.

* Reprinted with permission, 1984 *Crayola Dream-makers Program*, Binney & Smith, Inc.

Bulletin Board 4

Learning the Skills of Peacemaking

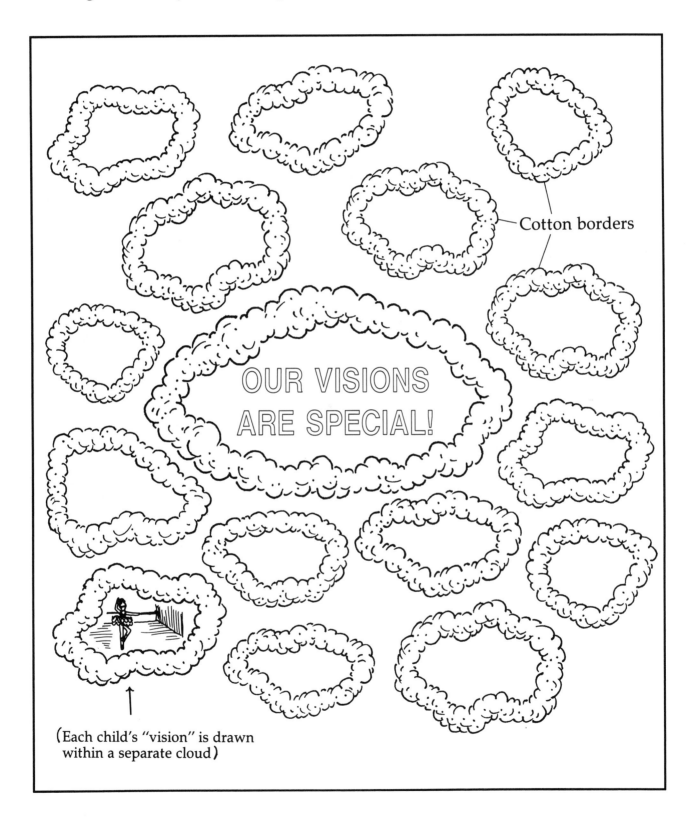

OUR VISIONS
ARE SPECIAL!

Cotton borders

(Each child's "vision" is drawn
within a separate cloud)

OUR VISION OF A PEACEFUL SCHOOL

OBJECTIVES

- The children will think about what their school would be like if it were totally peaceful.
- The children will draw distinctions between qualities of a peaceful and non-peaceful school.
- The children will collaborate on group murals of a "peaceful school."

  NOTE: This lesson correlates with Bulletin Board 5 entitled "A Peaceful School Looks Like This."

MATERIALS

- Two pieces of poster paper with the headings:

  A Non-Peaceful School

  A Peaceful School
- Large sheets of mural paper—one for every group of five children
- Markers, crayons, any other art materials that can be used in creating a mural
- Logs

PROCEDURE

1. Have the children sit in a circle. State, "We have talked about how peace starts with us, and we've talked about our ideas. Today we're going to combine these ideas and think about what it would be like to have a school that's totally peaceful, and the part we can play in making it that way.

2. Say, "The first thing I'm going to ask you to think about is the opposite of a peaceful school." Direct your class's attention to the poster, "A Non-Peaceful School." Ask your students to think for a moment of the way their school or any other school is when it's not peaceful. Say, "How do the people in the school treat each other in a non-peaceful setting? How does it feel?"

3. List the qualities of a non-peaceful school on the poster and discuss them.

4. Say, "Now let's think about a school that is perfectly peaceful. Think about a school that is exactly the way you want it to be. No idea is too outrageous, so please don't limit your thoughts or judge them. Often the most creative ideas come out of thoughts we label as 'silly' or 'unrealistic.' The opportunity today is to allow yourself the freedom to think of whatever you

choose." Allow time for questions and brief discussion.

5. "Imagine what your school would look like if you could have it exactly the very way you want it to be." Give the class a minute of complete silence in which to do this.

6. Say, "Now, picture people coming into your peaceful school. How do their faces look? How are they treating each other? Listen to their voices. How do they sound? What's it like in the halls and lunchroom and on the playground? Think about your teacher. How are your teacher and the children relating to one another?"

7. Ask, "Are there any other people around? Adults? Parents? Are there any pets or animals? How do you feel in this school?" Give the children another minute or two to think about this quietly.

8. Ask, "What was it like to think about a peaceful school?" Discuss. Encourage the students to describe the different aspects of their ideas. List portions of their descriptions on the poster entitled "A Peaceful School."

9. After discussion have the class break up into teams of five. Give each team the large mural paper, markers, and crayons.

10. Say, "We're going to combine our individual ideas into group ideas. Take a few minutes to plan the creation of a mural of a peaceful school and its surrounding area. Decide who will draw the different parts. You'll be sharing the crayons and drawing materials together in each group. If you have a conflict, use the Win/Win Guidelines to work it out. Your job is to develop and complete your murals cooperatively in about twenty minutes. Any questions?"

11. Have students work in groups as you circulate. Note the processes they use to determine the content and development of their mural. Be available to help them mediate differences, but don't have them lean on you too heavily.

12. At the end of the lesson, have each group describe their mural to the class. Ask them also to describe the process they used to determine how the mural would be done. Ask if there were any conflicts and how they were handled.

13. State, "A peaceful world is dependent on people like you working together on many different projects. How can we as individuals take responsibility for working well together?" Discuss. "How can we as individuals have our school become the peaceful place we have thought about?" Guide your students to take on specific responsibilities in this regard. For example, children might state, "I'll work out my conflicts rather than fighting," or "I'll pick up litter in and around the school," or "If someone new comes to our school, I'll make friends with them so they're not alone."

14. Have the children respond to this lesson in their logs.

Bulletin Board 5
Learning the Skills of Peacemaking

A PEACEFUL SCHOOL LOOKS LIKE THIS...

Children's "Group Mural"

Paper border

THE NICEST THING ABOUT. . .

OBJECTIVES

- The children will appreciate the special goodness in others.
- The children will observe, compare, and evaluate the positive qualities in their classmates.

     NOTE: This lesson correlates with Bulletin Board 6 entitled "The Nicest Thing About ..."

MATERIALS

- 3 x 5 index cards
- Paper, crayons or magic markers
- Large face cut-out
- Yarn (different colors), one for each child
- 4 x 6 white or manila paper
- scissors

PROCEDURE

1. Say, "Remember how we discussed peace starting with each individual. Remember how we as individuals created our idea of a peaceful school. Part of being peaceful is accepting and affirming one another. In today's lesson we're going to choose one person in our class we will affirm in a very special way."

2. Discuss with the children how each child has a special kind of goodness inside.

3. Choose one child to come forward.

     NOTE: This lesson is to be repeated every week or so until every child in the class has had a chance to be the focus.

4. Distribute the 3 x 5 cards to every member of the class. Have each child write the name of the person you just selected on the top of the card. Their own name goes at the bottom.

5. Tell the children that the cards will be used after our discussion when each person can write one special quality on the card about the person in front of the room. Tell the children that the cards will go on the bulletin board entitled "The Nicest Thing About..."

6. Ask the class to tell you what the special qualities are about the person selected. Discuss.

7. After the discussion is complete, have each child write on the 3 x 5 card a sentence expressing something about the special quality of the child in front of the room. For example, "Kenny is funny and he tells good jokes and makes me laugh." Next, have each child draw and cut out a picture of his/her own face on the 4 x 6 paper.

     NOTE: For young children you will need an aide or helper to complete this part of the lesson.

8. While the class is working, give the large face cut-out to the selected child. Have the child draw his/her own face and hair on the cut-out.

9. Put the large face on the bulletin board. Hang each note card and small 4 x 6 picture around the face. Connect the yarn from each note card to the large face.

10. If you have access to a camera, take a picture of this bulletin board and send it home with the selected child.

Bulletin Board 6
Learning the Skills of Peacemaking

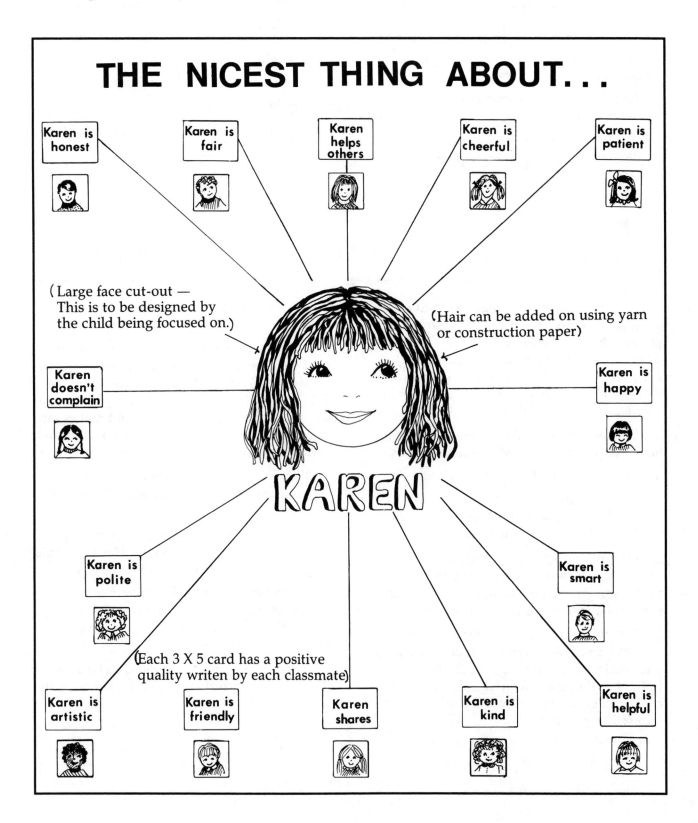

THE NICEST THING ABOUT...

Karen is honest

Karen is fair

Karen helps others

Karen is cheerful

Karen is patient

(Large face cut-out — This is to be designed by the child being focused on.)

(Hair can be added on using yarn or construction paper)

Karen doesn't complain

Karen is happy

KAREN

Karen is polite

Karen is smart

(Each 3 X 5 card has a positive quality writen by each classmate)

Karen is artistic

Karen is friendly

Karen shares

Karen is kind

Karen is helpful

BEING DIFFERENT IS OK

OBJECTIVES

- The children will develop a deeper understanding that all people have ways they are different from one another, but each individual is unique and special.

- The children will learn the value of being different.

- The children will develop a deeper understanding of the importance of accepting differences in others.

MATERIALS

- Poster with the following quote:

> "It has often proved true that the dream of yesterday is the hope of today and the reality of tomorrow."
>
> Robert Hutchings Goddard

- "The Dream of Unknown Worlds," Robert Hutchings Goddard (see page 148)

- Diorama materials: shoe boxes, paste, scissors, crayons, pipe cleaners, clay, clothespins, etc.

PROCEDURE

1. Have the children form a circle and do some slow, quiet, deep breathing. Have the children listen to the quietness in the classroom and feel the calmness within themselves.

2. Say, "Everything of value that has ever been created by human beings has come from somebody's dream. It is possible for us to make our dreams become a reality." Discuss this concept and allow for questions. Say, "Now I'm going to read a very special quote from a very special person named Robert Hutchings Goddard, whose dream has changed all of our lives." Read the quote on the poster: "It has often proved true that the dream of yesterday is the hope of today and the reality of tomorrow." Explain this thoroughly to the children, and make sure they understand it before going on.

3. Tell the children that you're going to read them a story about Robert Hutchings Goddard and his special dream, but first go over the following points:

a. We all have dreams.

b. Our dreams are special.

c. Nothing is too outrageous to think about.

d. All of the wonderful achievements in the world have sprung from the dreams of people like us.

4. Say, "I'm going to read you the story of Robert Hutchings Goddard, who had a dream people considered to be so outrageous that they called him the 'Moon Man,' but that didn't stop him from making his dream a reality."

5. Read the text on page 148, "The Dream of Unknown Worlds," and discuss it.

6. Ask the children, "Do you ever feel different? How?" Discuss, and as you listen, keep reinforcing that each child is special, and that it's fine to be different. Also reinforce that it's important to accept differences in others, and that part of peacemaking is the acceptance of differences.

7. Ask, "How would our world be different today if Robert Hutchings Goddard had given up his dream when people made fun of him?" Discuss. Keep reinforcing Goddard's courage and the importance of his dream and his willingness to take a stand in the face of obstacles. Discuss taking a stand. Tell the children what that means to you. Ask what it means to them.

8. Ask, "Have you ever given up a dream because of what other people have said?" This is a good time to share a personal anecdote about a dream you gave up because of someone else's attitude or negative response.

9. Ask, "How can we encourage one another's dreams?" Stress the value of acceptance, support, and caring for others.

10. Say, "Many of us have dreams of making the world a better place. What is your dream of making the world a better place? What types of changes would you make?" Share your dream first. Have the children discuss ways in which they think about making the world a better place.

11. Have the children make dioramas entitled "My Dream of Making the World a Better Place." This can be done at home or in school using shoe boxes or gift-sized boxes and mixed-media materials (fabric, pipe-cleaners, clay, magazine pictures, clothespins, paste, crayons, etc.)

12. Follow-up: When the dioramas are complete, have each child discuss their diorama and the dream it expresses. Dioramas can be displayed in the school library or another visible place in the school. Invite another class to see the dioramas and hear about the dreams which inspired them.

THE DREAM OF UNKNOWN WORLDS

Robert Hutchings Goddard (1882-1945)*

People teased young Robert Goddard about being weird: he was really crazy about machines. As soon as he could talk, he started asking scientific questions. He tried experiments, too. Once he made a balloon with helium, but it failed to rise off the ground.

Robert was always daydreaming about faraway places and unknown worlds. His favorite story was The War of the Worlds about an invasion from Mars.

One of Robert's own daydreams was so vivid that it seemed real to him. It happened when he was 17 years old. He was climbing a cherry tree in his grandmother's orchard to prune a dead limb. He looked into the sky. Suddenly he imagined he was in a flying machine. The machine had some sort of device that allowed it to escape the pull of gravity and soar off into space. Robert felt as if he were flying to the moon!

Robert spent the rest of his life trying to make this daydream come true. First he studied physics, the science of energy and motion. Then he started building his own rockets and shooting them off. The launching began to attract attention. People thought Goddard was crazy. The newspapers called him the "Moon Man." His home state of Massachusetts even banned his launchings there, for fear they would cause brush fires!

Goddard had other problems, too. He was often sick. His body was thin and frail. For most of his life he suffered from tuberculosis. But Goddard didn't give up. He finally found a few other people who believed in his dream and that helped him to continue his experiments.

Many of his experiments were failures. He never came close to getting a rocket to the moon. The moon is 240,000 miles away. Goddard's greatest rocket went only 9,000 feet up—not quite two miles. Nevertheless, Robert Goddard is known as the father of modern rocketry. He took out patents for 200 rocketry inventions. Two of his discoveries were especially important. There is hardly any air in outer space: it is nearly a vacuum. Goddard was the first to prove that a rocket could fly within a vacuum. He also discovered the first solid rocket fuel which makes today's space travel possible.

When Goddard died in 1945, he still believed in his dream of unknown worlds. He was sure that people would fly to the moon.

* Reprinted with permission, 1984 *Crayola Dream-maker Program*, Binney & Smith, Inc.

OTHER PEOPLE ARE DIFFERENT TOO

OBJECTIVES

- The children will explore attitudes toward differences in others.
- The children will pinpoint specific differences to which they have reacted in the past (racial, gender, ethnic, age, handicap, religious, other).
- The children will learn that as peacemakers they need to accept the differences in others.
- The children will collaborate on a group mural.

    NOTE: This lesson correlates with Bulletin Board 7 entitled "We Celebrate Our Differences."

MATERIALS

- Poem: "Kids Are Different" (see page 151)
- *National Geographic* or another magazine which has pictures of people of different races, colors, ethnic origins, ages, genders. Pictures of handicapped people are very appropriate also. These magazines will be used for cutting up.
- Paste, scissors
- Large mural paper with heading: "We Celebrate Our Differences." The paper should be large enough for each child in the class to paste several pictures on. Make sure the mural paper will fit on your bulletin board.

PROCEDURE

1.   Have the children sit in a circle. Do some deep breathing, and read the poem, "Kids Are Different." Discuss the concept of human differences. Ask what kinds of human differences were referred to in the poem. Ask, "How do you feel when you're with people who are different from you?" Discuss. Ask, "Is it okay for people to be different, or would it be better if we were all the same?" Discuss. On the board, write the terms: ethnic, racial, gender, handicap, religion. Describe the meaning of each term and ask the children how people seem to react to these differences in others. Discuss.

2.   Have each of the children turn to the person they are sitting next to.

3.   Say, "Look at your partner. How is he/she different from you?" Discuss this together. Acknowledge each person who speaks.

4.   Ask, "What differences did you notice in your partner?" Discuss and keep reiterating that we all differ from one another in many ways. Acknowledge each person who speaks.

5.   Ask, "Have you ever seen or known someone who was different than you? How did those differences make you feel?" Discuss and stress that it is okay to have feelings, whatever they may be. Ultimately it is our actions that make a difference. Children may feel awkward or guilty about being put off by differences. Let them know that they are not alone in feeling this way, but that the process of learning to value each individual as special and unique is an important one.

6.   Say, "We are all different in some way. How does it make you feel when someone puts you down for being different?"

7.   Ask, "If we want to create a peaceful world, how can we treat people who we perceive as being different? Remember, we are all different in some way. How are you different?" Discuss. Guide the students to understand the value of taking responsibility for their actions and attitudes, as well as the importance of accepting others.

8. Say, "If we want a world at peace, then we must start, as individuals, with an attitude of acceptance and understanding. Can we expect nations of the world to accept one another's differences if we cannot be accepting as individuals?" Discuss. Reiterate that we are all the same inside.

9. Reiterate that peace starts with the individual.

10. Have your students work in small groups, locating and cutting out pictures of people of different colors, races, ages, genders, etc. Encourage your students to discuss the concept of acceptance of human differences as they work.

11. Remind your students that this is a collaborative activity. Explain the meaning of the word "collaborative." State, "If we're each going to take full responsibility for having the kind of world we want, then we must find ways to work collaboratively in large and small groups.

12. Direct attention to the mural paper entitled "We Celebrate Our Differences." Have the class paste their pictures on the mural paper. Encourage them to work out ways to take turns and not get in each other's way. Note the process the children use to do this, and discuss the process with them. Note what works and what doesn't work. Discuss.

13. Conclude by guiding the students to reiterate the value of being different and accepting differences in others. Finally, stress again that peace starts with the individual and that each person's actions make an impact on the world.

KIDS ARE DIFFERENT

Kids are diff'rent
We don't even look the same
Some kids speak different languages
We all have a different name
Kids are different
But if you look inside you'll see
That tall kid, that small kid
Is just like you and me.
Some folks are surprised that
Kids in wheelchairs play
Blind kids read, deaf kids talk
Except in a different way.
Able kids, disabled kids
There's nothing we can't do
Just take a look inside yourself
You'll be so proud of you
Because
Kids are diff'rent
We don't even look the same
Some kids speak different languages
We all have a different name.
Kids are different
But if you look inside you'll see
That tall kid, that small kid
That deaf kid, that blind kid
Is just like you and me.

From *"Kids on the Block."* Lyrics, Barbara Aiello; Music, Bud Forrest. Permission to reprint granted to all who wish to reproduce the words to this song.

Bulletin Board 7
Learning the Skills of Peacemaking

WE CELEBRATE OUR DIFFERENCES!

Collage of magazine pictures
indicating human differences

(Paper border)

OUR FEELINGS ARE OK

OBJECTIVES

- The children will learn that people all have a variety of different feelings.

- The children will understand that it's important to accept their own feelings and the feelings of others.

- The children will understand that human beings must be responsible for "owning" their feelings and actions, and that they can choose their actions.

- The children will practice using "I messages."

MATERIALS

- Optional: From the book *Free To Be You And Me*, the story, "It's Alright To Cry"

- Pictures of people showing emotion (happiness, sadness, anger, surprise, fear). You can have the children bring these in ahead of time.

- Large mural paper entitled: "All Kinds of Feelings"

- Markers (for grades 2-6)

- Large poster with the words: Accept Your Feelings, and Choose Your Actions Wisely.

PROCEDURE

1. Have the children form a circle. If you have the book, *Free To Be You And Me*, read the story "It's Alright To Cry." Discuss the feelings of sadness expressed by the main character. This is optional. If you do not have the book, ask students to share about a time they've felt sad about something. Have several people share.

2. Ask the students to share the way they feel right now. Accept any answer. Encourage full participation.

3. Show pictures of people with different feelings. Discuss.

4. Show the children the mural paper entitled: "All Kinds of Feelings." Ask them to tell you about the different feelings they have experienced. Place the paper on the floor and give each child a marker. Ask the students to write down any feeling they have ever had. Give them five to ten minutes. Younger children can illustrate the feelings using pictures of facial expressions.

5. After the time has elapsed, have the children form a circle. Tell them, "Feelings are a natural part of who we are." Refer to the poster: "Accept Your Feelings, and Choose Your

Actions Wisely." Say, "What does this mean?" Discuss. Stress the concept that people can choose how they want to act. Example: "Just because someone is angry, that person doesn't have to hit. He or she can choose to express feelings in another way."

6. State, "Part of being a responsible member of the human family is realizing that we are the owners of our feelings. No one else can put feelings inside us. Other people can trigger our feelings, but ultimately the feelings are our own."

7. Say, "Each of us is whole and special and wonderful, even when we are angry or resentful. We don't become the feelings we are experiencing. When we feel angry, we are not bad, just angry. We must remember above all that we decide how we're going to act, and we must choose our actions carefully, always considering the feelings of others." Discuss alternatives for the expression of anger. Say, "What are some of the things you can do when you're angry so you don't hurt anyone?"

8. Hang up the poster "Accept Your Feelings" in the front of the room. Group the children into pairs. Ask each pair to complete these sentences, taking turns.

I feel happy when _____

I feel sad when _____

I feel angry when _____

I feel scared when _____

I feel great when _____

Discuss.

9. Say, "When we have conflicts with other people, lots of different feelings can surface. You may feel angry, frightened, frustrated, or sad." Give a personal example. Ask, "Have any of you had any recent conflicts you would like to share?" Ask the children to describe how they felt during the conflict.

10. Choose a conflict to have children act out. Ask for volunteers to play the parts of the various "characters," but don't use real names. Review the Win/Win Guidelines.

11. Have the volunteers play act a conflict in the center of the room. Coach them in stating feelings with "I messages."

12. When the play acting is complete, ask, "Do you think the things you're learning about feelings and conflicts can help you get along with others?" Discuss.

13. Stress that each time the children choose to work out their differences non-violently, they are helping to make the world more peaceful. Say, "Imagine what it would be like if everyone resolved their conflicts without the use of violence. What would the world be like?" Have the children share their responses.

MY FRIEND IS DIFFERENT AND HE/SHE IS SPECIAL

OBJECTIVES

- The children will understand that human differences make people unique and special.
- The children will reiterate the need for accepting others and valuing their uniqueness.
- The children will begin booklets entitled, "My Friend Is Different and He/She Is Special."

MATERIALS

- Large poster entitled:

> **"ABOUT HUMAN DIFFERENCES"**
> 1. Human beings are different in many ways, but we're all the same inside.
> 2. All people have the same basic needs: food, clothing, shelter, and love.
> 3. Our differences make us special and unique.
> 4. Peacemaking means accepting ourselves and others.
> 5. Affirming others for their uniqueness is important.
> 6. We all are interconnected regardless of our differences.

- Construction paper (9" x 12") for front/back cover of booklets
- Five or more pieces of drawing or writing paper per child (or five "My Friend Is Different and He/She Is Special" booklets — see page 157)
- Crayons, pencils, markers
- Chart entitled: "Human Beings Are Different and Special in Many Ways"

PROCEDURE

1. Have the children sit in a circle. Ask, "What did you learn about human differences in other lessons we have done?"

2. Show the poster "About Human Differences" and discuss the concepts. Guide the children to restate the concepts on the chart, in their own words, by asking what each sentence means.

3. Say, "Think about your friends. Think about how they are different from you. Think about your best friend. What is different about him or her? What is special?" Discuss.

4. Have the children turn to the person they're sitting next to for paired sharing.

5. Say, "We're going to take a few moments to tell our partners about a friend we have who is both different and special. You can start with an example of someone in your own life: for example, you could say, 'My friend is also very special because she's kind and smart.'" Give the class about four minutes to share in pairs.

6. Distribute papers for booklets. Younger children can illustrate the contents of the booklet. Older children can draw and write. Say,

"We're going to think of five people we know who are different and special. On each page you will draw/write what's different about them and what's special." [You can reproduce the text on page 157 for student booklets.] Again, stress the value of accepting human differences and the fact that we're all the same inside.

7. Follow-up: Have each child share his/her booklet with the class, describing the friends they wrote and drew about.

NOTE: The booklet can be completed at home, rather than in class. Be sure to have the children present their booklets to one another as oral reports when they are finished. This will be a great time to invite the parents in.

MY FRIEND IS DIFFERENT AND HE/SHE IS SPECIAL

Name:

Date:

Directions: Choose five people. On each page, write their first name and fill out the following:

My friend's name is:

He/She is different because:

He/She is special because:

Draw a picture of your special friend.

HUMAN DIFFERENCES: BEING JAIME

OBJECTIVES

- The children will put themselves in the place of someone who is "the different one."
- The children will develop an understanding of other people's reactions to differences.
- The children will develop an understanding of what it would be like to be the object of prejudice.

MATERIALS

- Poster: "About Human Differences"
- Drawing paper, crayons, or markers
- Peacemaking Logs

PROCEDURE

NOTE: Be sure to exercise extreme sensitivity in doing this lesson. Read "Being Jaime" to yourself first (below). If there are children in your class whose lives resemble Jaime's, decide ahead of time how to handle the presentation of the lesson.

1. Have the children form a circle. Review the poster from Lesson 39, "About Human Differences." Say, "We have discussed differences and what it is like to be the different one. Today we are going to imagine what it would be like to be a child named Jaime who is different than many of the other children in the school. As I read the story about Jaime I want you to imagine that you are Jaime. Jaime can be either a boy or a girl."

BEING JAIME

Jaime is nine years old. Jaime and his/her mother live with an aunt in a tiny apartment over an old hardware store. Jaime's mother cleans other people's homes for a living. She has very little money to buy clothes for Jaime, so Jaime has to wear old hand-me-downs. Jaime goes to school in a neighborhood where all the other children have nice clothes and live in big houses with pretty lawns. Imagine that you are Jaime. What would your life be like? How is Jaime's life like yours? How is it different?

---

2. Say, "Continue to imagine yourselves as Jaime. Picture yourself living with your mother and aunt in the tiny apartment above the hardware store. You have very few toys and the television is broken. Mom doesn't make enough money to get it fixed. You are cold because there has been no heat in your apartment this week. It's time for school. You put on your best outfit, but there is a rip in the sleeve. Your sneakers are old and the laces are broken and knotted in different places. You go outside to walk to school. You see other children walking in small groups, laughing and talking together. How do they act when they see you? What do they say? How do you feel? You get to school and go inside. The children continue to talk and laugh. They discuss the shows they watched on television last night. You walk through the crowd of children and go to your seat in the back of the room. You wait for the teacher to take attendance. How do the other children look at you? What do they say? How do you feel? What do you want to do? What do you wish the other children would do?" Allow a few moments of silence.

3. Say, "How did you feel being Jaime?" Discuss.

4. Ask, "How would your life be different from the way it is now if you were Jaime? Have you ever known anyone like Jaime? Have you ever felt like Jaime might feel?" Give the children ample time to discuss.

5. Say, "If we want to have a world in which people accept and cooperate with one another, how should we treat people who appear to be different than we are?"

6. State, "Remember, we always have a choice. As human beings, it is our responsibility to choose our actions carefully and appropriately. How can the actions chosen by the children around Jaime make Jaime's life a happier one?"

7. State, "Are you willing to make a commitment to being accepting of others?" Review the meaning of the word "commitment."

8. Say, "Imagine the different countries of the world treating each other with acceptance rather than non-acceptance. How would the world be different than it is now?"

9. Ask the children to draw Jaime's picture as he/she goes to school or is in class with the other children.

10. Have older children write in their logs about what it was like to be Jaime. Younger children can use drawing paper and crayons or markers to express their feelings.

DIFFERENT FLAGS OF DIFFERENT LANDS

OBJECTIVES

- The children will learn about different countries of the world through the use of pictures of flags.
- Each child will draw a flag of a different country.
- The children will begin research projects on the country associated with their flag.

MATERIALS

- Encyclopedias or dictionaries with pictures of flags; try to gather extras because the children will be copying the flags.
- Names of different countries printed on small squares of paper or notecards to be picked out of a box (have one country for each child)
- World map or globe
- Note to parents (see page 163)
- Research project contracts (see page 164)
- Construction paper, crayons, rulers, paint (optional), scissors and paste

  NOTE: You may want to make special arrangements with your school librarian before starting this project. It would be best to do a portion of this lesson in the library, so that each child can make a rough draft of his / her flag using books available there. It would also be helpful to have posted a chart with each child's name, country, and the due date of the project. You may want to give a brief overview of map skills before this lesson. The children will be locating various countries on the map or globe during the lesson.

PROCEDURE

1. Have the children form a circle. Say, "We know that our world is made up of many different kinds of people. Our differences make the world a more diverse [explain] and interesting place to live. We've talked about accepting differences. Sometimes it's easier to do this when we know more about the culture and background of other people. Today we're going to begin a project which will help us do just that." Show the encyclopedia or dictionary pages containing the flags of the world. Say: "Members of the human family come from many different countries throughout the world. We are all part of one world, one earth. These flags represent the different places in which the people of the world live."

2. Say, "Today we are each going to make a flag and choose a country to do a project on."

3. Say, "We're going to play a game called 'Pick a Country.'" Ask each child to close their eyes and pick the name of a country from a box. Have each child locate the country on the map or globe. Help the children find the country

they are looking for. (For remote countries, list the continent along with the country on each paper you place in the box.)

4.   After each child has found the country, say, "We are going to begin research projects about our different countries." Explain the meaning of "research project."

5.   Hand out the research project contracts. Go over them. Explain to the students that they can work with their parents on this project if they need help. Show them the letters for their parents.

6.   Have the children fill in the blanks of both the contract and the letter.

7.   Explain that the projects will help everyone learn more about the world in which they live. Say, "We will be finding out about other people with whom we share our planet."

NOTE: The portion of the lesson that can be done in the library follows.

8.   Say, "Let's begin by making a practice drawing of the flag of each of our countries." Distribute the dictionaries and encyclopedias and have the children do their practice copies. Tell the children they will make a larger flag with construction paper, paste, crayons, and markers. Say, "Draw and color carefully so that you can use your picture as a model."

9.   If there is enough time, have the children make their larger flag the same day. If not, this part of the lesson can be done the following day.

10. Say, "Remember, we are all interconnected; we are connected to all the other people on earth as a human family." Reiterate how their projects will help the students learn about people with whom they share the earth.

NOTE TO PARENTS
Learning the Skills of Peacemaking
Lesson 41

Dear Parents:

As part of *Learning the Skills of Peacemaking*, your child has brought home a picture of a flag he/she has created from _____. He/she has been asked to

country

complete a research project on that country. Would you assist your child in finding the following information:

1. location of country
2. map of country (student draws this)
3. population
4. traditional foods
5. most common jobs
6. native dwelling (describe, draw, or make model of, if available)
7. other interesting facts

Your child should write, in his/her own words, a report on his/her country including the above information. Although this project should be done by your child, your assistance and guidance will be most helpful. Please contact me if there are any questions. I would be happy to discuss them with you.

Sincerely,

Teacher's Name _____

Due Date _____

Student's Name _____

· Tear Off and Return ·

I _____ agree to help my child _____
(Parent)   (Name)

complete his/her research project by _____.

Signature _____

RESEARCH PROJECT CONTRACT
Learning the Skills of Peacemaking
Lesson 41

I, _____, agree to be responsible for the
　　　　　　　　(Student's name)

completion of my research project on _____ by
　　　　　　　　　　　　　　　　　　　　　　　(Country)

_____ .
　　　　　(Due date)

I agree to get the help I need in order to finish carefully and on time. I agree to meet
with my teacher if I have a problem.

_____　　_____
Signature of Student　　　　　　　　　　　Date

DIFFERENT FLAGS: ORAL REPORTS

OBJECTIVES

- The children will present their research projects orally.
- The children will each "become the teacher" during his/her presentation. They can use the map, globe, pointer, and any other visuals they request.

  NOTE: For this lesson, older children can make their own transparencies for their presentation and use the overhead projector. Students may also enjoy using the opaque projector. Encourage them to bring in any other visuals they might have or can create relating to their projects.

MATERIALS

- Research projects
- Maps, globes, pointer
- Projector (optional)
- Tape recorder to record each child's report (optional)
- Optional: a baked or cooked "treat" from the countries being reported on

PROCEDURE

1. Children present research projects, one at a time, in front of the class. They locate their country on the map or globe. Each child's flag should be displayed when they are giving their reports. Any other visuals should be shown at this time.

2. Discuss each report briefly. Encourage children to draw comparisons among the countries. Optional: Tape record each report.

Children can listen to themselves with headphones during free time.

3. Display all reports and visuals.

4. Invite another class in to see the displayed reports and flags. Each child in your class can tell the other children what country they worked on.

TAKING PART IN OUR COMMUNITIES

OBJECTIVES

- The children will choose a community or school problem on which they would like to focus.

- The children will brainstorm solutions to this problem in small groups.

- The children will choose a solution and describe a plan of action.

    NOTE: First grade teachers will need the assistance of parents, aides, or several children from a higher grade to help record brainstorming ideas.

MATERIALS

- Brainstorming Poster from Lesson 14
- Large Poster entitled "Things Needing Improvement"
- One piece of chart paper and marker for each group
- Peacekeeping Logs

PROCEDURE

1. Have the students form a circle. Tell them that this lesson will focus on thinking about solutions to community or school problems. Ask the class to choose whether they want to focus on the community or the school.

2. After the decision is made, ask the students to think of things they see in need of improvement or change. (For example, a school problem might be litter on the playground. A community problem might be the need for low-cost housing.)

3. Record suggested problem areas on the "Things Needing Improvement" poster.

4. After a sufficient amount of suggestions have been made, the class can vote on the problem which they would like to focus on.

5. Review the Brainstorming Poster thoroughly. Say, "Today we're going to use the process of brainstorming to come up with solutions to the problem we've just discussed."

6. Have the children break up into "problem-solving groups" of four or five. They pick a leader. Explain that the leader records the ideas of the group. Pass out the chart paper and markers. Say, "Take five to ten minutes and

brainstorm all the ideas you can. Remember, everybody has good ideas and everybody's ideas are worthwhile." (For young children, the helper will record.)

7. Allow the children five to ten minutes to brainstorm solutions.

8. Stop the discussion after ten minutes and ask the children to decide on one solution per group. This should take about five minutes. Remind them to use the Win/Win Guidelines when needed.

9. Ask the group leaders to share the solutions his/her group came up with. Then have the class vote on the best solution.

10. Once the solution has been agreed upon, say, "We now need to implement a plan of action." Talk about specific steps that can be taken to address the problem. For example, if the students focused on a school problem, they can write letters to the principal describing the problem and outlining their solutions. Or perhaps a group of students will visit the principal to discuss the class's concern about the problem, and to let him or her know of their suggested solution. For community problems, the class can write or phone the mayor or town council, write

a letter to the local newspaper, or come up with their own way of solving the problem.

11. Follow-up: Have students in grades 2-6 expand on this topic in their log books. The entry can be entitled "How I Can Make a Difference in My School or Community." The students can describe another problem they are aware of, listing possible solutions. They can come up with ideas about what kids can do to deal with the problem. (Younger students can illustrate the problem on one page and the solution on another in their logs.)

SENTENCE WRITING USING FAMILIAR TERMS

OBJECTIVES

- The children will discuss the meaning of new terms used in past lessons.

- The children will re-state the meaning of each term.

- The children will use these terms in a sentence, either oral or written, to show that they understand the meaning.

  NOTE: Teachers from Grade 1 who want to use this lesson can discuss and review the meaning of each term, rather than have the children write them. I was able to eventually have my first graders write sentences using the terms. In fact they loved the idea of using and understanding "grown-up" words. I laughed with one parent when she told me how her six-year-old came home and asked her to "affirm" him.

MATERIALS

- Large chart entitled "Peacemaking Terms" (see page 170)

- Paper and pencils

PROCEDURE

1. Have the children sit in a circle.

2. Direct their attention to the poster, "Peacemaking Terms." Go around the circle and have the children talk about each term. Discuss the meanings together. Help the class clear up any misunderstandings they have about each term.

3. Divide the list of terms into groups of five or six words. On selected days have your students write the definitions of each term and then use each term in a sentence.

4. Have the children work as partners. Those who need extra assistance can work with others who have a better grasp of the meaning and use of each term. Stress the value of cooperation and helping one another.

PEACEMAKING TERMS

cooperate
conflict
resolution
affirm
acknowledge
peace
ethnic
racial
handicap
gender
unique
brainstorm
reality
interconnected
I Message
Win/Win
well-being
peacemaker
contribution
problem-solving
commitment
considerate
responsibility
integrity
morals
consequences

CONFLICTS IN THE NEWS

NOTE: Send home Current Events Letters to Parents from Lesson 32 ahead of time and before proceeding.

OBJECTIVES

- The children will each bring in a current events article focusing on a conflict at any level (interpersonal, local, global).

- The children will use brainstorming to come up with solutions for a conflict in the news.

- The children will understand that they have the ability to express themselves and "make a difference," regardless of their age.

  NOTE: This lesson correlates with Bulletin Board 8 entitled: "Problems in the News: Kids Have the Answers!"

MATERIALS

- Current events article about a conflict of some kind. (Each child should be asked to bring one in ahead of time.)

- Win/Win Guidelines

- Large chart paper and marker for each problem-solving group of five students

- 5" x 7" piece of paper for each child to cut out into face shape and draw his/her face on

- Crayons/markers to color face cut-outs

- Scissors

PROCEDURE

1. Have the children sit in a circle with their current events articles. Say, "Just as we have the ability to make a difference and express our opinions about school and community issues, we can also express ourselves about national and global issues, particularly in regard to issues appearing in the news."

2. Say, "Today we're going to examine some articles you have brought in from the newspapers or magazines. We're going to go around the circle and I'd like each person to tell in a few sentences what his or her article is about."

3. Have each child briefly describe his/her article and state the conflict represented within.

4. After each child has spoken, choose one article on which to focus. Read or paraphrase it for the class and then have the class restate the

conflict situation. On the board, write a sentence expressing the conflict.

5. Direct the students' attention to the Win/Win Guidelines. Review them and ask the children to think about how the guidelines can be applied to the conflict in the article. Discuss.

6. Have the class divide into problem-solving groups of four or five. Ask each group to choose a leader who will record the suggestions of his/her teammates on chart paper. (Here's where first graders will need the help of parents, aides, or older children. The leader can ask for ideas, and the helper will record.) Encourage the students to choose people who have not been a leader before.

7. Ask the children to think of the Win/Win Guidelines in discussing the conflict in the

article. Ask them to give particular attention to "brainstorming" solutions. Remind them that no solution is too outrageous to state. Encourage them to be as creative as possible when brainstorming. Let them know that they will eventually choose only one or two solutions (perhaps combining several), and that the creative process will unlock new ideas.

8. Say, "I am going to give you seven to ten minutes to generate your ideas and decide on a solution." Distribute the chart paper and markers to each group. Be sure the Win/Win Guidelines are available for reference. Observe how the students apply the process, and be available to mediate differences. Encourage them to be sensitive to the feelings of people on both sides of the conflict represented in the article.

9. After the allotted time, have each group leader present the solution decided upon and comment on how the problem-solving process was used in the group.

10. Write the solution presented by each group on the board. Have the students vote on which solution they would like to support as a class.

11. Write a class letter to the newspaper or magazine from which the article was taken and outline the solution.

12. Distribute the 5" x 7" pieces of paper and have each child draw and color his/her face, and cut it out. Tell the children that their "faces" will go on the "Problems in the News: Kids Have the Answers!" bulletin board.

13. During the month, be sure to look in the "Letters" section of the newspaper or magazine for your class's letter. When the letter is printed, copy it and give one to each member of the class to take home.

14. Be sure to hang the printed letter on the bulletin board. If the letter doesn't get in the paper, hang your own copy of it on the bulletin board. Stress to the class that their ideas make a difference. State, "No matter how young or old you are, you have the ability to make a difference in the world. You can express yourselves to the newspapers and elected officials on any issue you feel is important."

NOTE: A sample Letter to the Editor is presented below. The conflict addressed was the burning of a house owned by a black family in a white neighborhood and the desecration of a temple in the same neighborhood.

LETTER TO THE EDITOR

Dear Editor:

Being kind to others is very important. We feel badly that a house was burnt down in the development near our school. We heard this happened because the family had a different color skin. We believe we should be kind to people of different colors and religions. We also feel bad that the temple has a hole in it. We think everybody should be kind to one another. We want to live in a peaceful world. This earth is a good place to be. Even if you're a German, Israeli, Indian, it doesn't matter where you come from. It does matter how you act. It doesn't matter where you come from or how you look. You are a part of this world. We're sorry that people got killed in wars. Please be kind to one another.

Sincerely,

Mrs. Drew's First Grade

NOTE: Be sure to include the name of every child in your class when you do this. This will be a priceless and long-remembered experience for all of them, and for those who read the letter.

Bulletin Board 8
Learning the Skills of Peacemaking

FINDING THE PEACEMAKERS

NOTE: Be sure to send home in advance the Letter to Parents at the end of this lesson.

OBJECTIVES

- The children will describe the qualities of peacemakers in the articles, stories, and pictures they have brought in.
- The children will practice reflective listening.
- The children will collaboratively create pictures of peacemakers.

    NOTE: This lesson correlates with Bulletin Board 9 entitled "Peacemakers in Our World."

MATERIALS

- Letter to Parents to be given out prior to the lesson (see page 176)
- Current events articles, books, and stories children have brought in describing peace-makers
- "A Peacemaker Is Someone Who..." poster from Lesson 21
- Peacemaking Logs

PROCEDURE

1. Ask the children to bring their articles, books, and stories on peacemakers to the circle.

2. Go over the "A Peacemaker Is Someone Who..." poster.

3. Have each of the children turn toward the person they are sitting next to for "paired sharing."

4. Say, "Each of you is going to tell your partner about the peacemaker in your article, book, or story. We'll take about five minutes to share, and then you will each tell the class about your partner's peacemaker. Remember to listen carefully while your partner speaks."

5. Give the class five to six minutes for paired sharing.

6. Have each child tell briefly about his/her partner's peacemaker.

7. Have the partners select together the most interesting peacemaker they heard about today.

8. Ask the partners to draw a picture of that peacemaker together. Allow the children to figure out how they're going to do this. Each pair of children should end up with one picture on which they both worked.

9. Display the finished pictures on the bulletin board.

10. Have the children write about the process of working on the picture together, and the peace-maker they chose, in their logs. (Younger children can do illustrations.)

LETTER TO PARENTS

Dear Parents,

Your children have been asked to locate articles and pictures of people who are peacemakers in newspapers, magazines, and books. Will you please assist them in finding what they need and in going over the content of the article or story about the peacemakers they have selected. As always, thank you for your willingness to help.

Sincerely,

_____

Teacher

_____

Date

Bulletin Board 9
Learning the Skills of Peacemaking

PEACEMAKERS IN OUR WORLD

Ghandi

Martin Luther King

George Washington

Mother Theresa

 This bulletin board contains a combination of pictures and photos of peacemakers

Pictures can be hand-drawn and cut out. Captions should be placed beneath each picture.

BUILDING A "CIVILIZATION OF LOVE"

OBJECTIVES

- The children will define what a "Civilization of Love" means to them.

- The children will think about what a "Civilization of Love" would be like.

- The children will discuss the following concept: "respect for the unique dignity of each human being."

MATERIALS

- Large chart paper entitled "A Civilization of Love"

- Mural paper entitled "A Civilization of Love"

- Markers, paints, crayons, etc.

- Definitions on a poster for: unique, dignity, civilization, and respect

- Books on Gandhi (optional)

PROCEDURE

1. Have the class form a circle. Do the following exercise. Say, "Take some deep breaths. Imagine yourself walking into a room filled with people you don't know, but you feel perfectly safe and relaxed. It is a bright sunny room. The people are smiling and talking quietly. They smile at you and immediately start talking to you, just as if they had always known you. You feel perfectly comfortable. You know that these people care about you, even though they didn't know you before. You notice that the people have skin of different colors and different facial characteristics. Some are black, some white, some Asian, some Indian, some Hispanic. You begin to feel like they are your family. You feel safe, loved, and accepted in this room. You don't want to leave it. You know you are in a special place."

2. Have the children describe how they feel.

3. Tell them that you are now going to read them an excerpt from the newspaper of a statement by Pope John Paul. Let the class know that Pope John Paul is a peacemaker, and that in the article he talks about another famous peacemaker, perhaps the most famous one of all, Mahatma Gandhi.

4. Ask, "Who knows who Gandhi was and why people all over the world respect him so much?" Discuss and give some background on Gandhi. If you have a book on Gandhi show it now and display any photos.

5. Read the following newspaper excerpt once, then reread it, making sure that your class understands what you're reading. Go over the definitions and give all the explanation the children need. "Mahatma Gandhi taught that if all men and women, whatever the differences between them, cling to the truth, with respect for the unique dignity of every human being, a new world order—a civilization of love—can be achieved" (*The Star Ledger*, Newark, NJ; February 1, 1986).

6. Ask, "What would a 'civilization of love' be like?" Share your own feelings about this.

7. Go around the circle and have the children give their interpretations and feelings.

8. Ask, "What does 'respect for the unique dignity of each human being' mean?" Discuss.

9. Have the children silently think about "a civilization of love where the unique dignity of every human being would be respected."

10 After about three minutes, have the children share what they thought about. Record the elements of their ideas: feelings, descriptions, etc. on the chart paper.

11. Put the mural paper entitled "A Civilization of Love" on the floor. Move the desks. Pass out the paints, etc. Let the children spread out and compose a mural together as a whole class. They should take about five minutes ahead of time to plan how they will do this.

12. Stress that this is a collaborative effort in which they will demonstrate the principles of peace and cooperation to which Gandhi dedicated his life.

13. Follow-up: Invite the principal to see the mural. Create an opportunity to display it to the parents. Call the local newspapers and ask them to take a picture of it with the class. Let the children know that, through their artistic expressions, they are making a huge difference, and they are sending a message to all the people who see their mural.

MEASURING THE UNDERSTANDINGS LEARNED IN THIS GUIDE

STAGE II: Integrating Peacemaking Into Our Lives

NOTE: You can use this page as a test of the understandings in Stage II, with age groups where this is appropriate. You can also use the questions to orally survey your students to find out their depth of understanding of the concepts covered.

1. What does "Peace starts with me" mean?

2. Explain the rules for brainstorming in your own words.

3. Why is brainstorming important?

4. What are some human differences? Please list some.

5. What are the different ways people keep informed?

6. Why is it important to keep informed?

7. List two well-known peacemakers and describe why they qualify as peacemakers.

8. What have you done in the past month to aid your school, community, or country?

9. Define:

   unique   morals

   dignity   integrity

   interconnected consequences

   respect

10. What are you doing to work out your conflicts with other people?

Stage III: Exploring Our Roots And Interconnectedness

"If civilization is to survive, we must culminate the science of human relationships—the ability of all peoples, of all kinds, to live together, in the same world at peace."

Franklin Delano Roosevelt

GROUP BRAINSTORMING – GLOBAL ISSUES

NOTE: Be sure to send home the Letter to Parents (found at the end of this lesson) before proceeding.

OBJECTIVES

- The students will summarize articles they have brought in about other countries, from newspapers or magazines.

- The students will determine the main issue or problem addressed in a selected article.

- The students will brainstorm solutions to the problem in a selected article.

- The students will work collaboratively to reach a conclusion.

- The students will decide upon a plan of action.

MATERIALS

- Student articles
- Map
- One piece of chart paper and marker for each group of five children
- Chalkboard, chalk

PROCEDURE

1.   Ask students to sit in a circle and bring their articles. Say, "All year long, we have been look-ing at how we can take part in having a more peaceful world. Today we're going to look at some global issues." Go over the words "global" and "issues." Say, "We're going to come up with a solution for at least one of the problems we read about."

2.   Ask, "Why is it important for us to know about global issues?" Discuss. Stress that all people are citizens—not only of their communi-ties, their states, and their countries, but also of the world. State, "We are all part of the human family." Ask, "What does being a part of the human family mean to you?"

3.   Review the meaning of "interconnected-ness." Ask: "How are we interconnected with the environment?" Discuss. Stress our depen-dency on air, light, food, and water. Ask, "How are we interconnected with one another?" Discuss.

4.   Say, "Today we're going to take a careful look at issues and problems of a global nature. We will listen to each other summarize our articles, and then we will focus on one article to brainstorm about."

5.   Have each child briefly summarize his/her article, indicating the names of the countries involved and what issue is being addressed.

6.   Choose one article on which to focus. Briefly review it and write the problem on the board. Have a child locate the country in the article on the map, naming the countries around it. Name the continent it is on. Have the class break up into problem-solving groups.

7.   Have each group choose a leader. The leader will record all brainstorming ideas on a piece of chart paper and share them later.

8.   Say, "I'm going to give you five to ten min-utes to brainstorm solutions to the problem in the article. Keep in mind the basic needs of the

people in the article. Put yourself in their place and think of what kind of solution you would most want." Distribute chart paper and markers.

9.   Give the class brainstorming time. When they have reached a conclusion, have the groups return to the circle, and allow time for each group leader to share solutions. Write the solutions on the board and put a check by the ones that are repeated.

10. Review the entire list of brainstorming solutions. Have the class choose the best ones. Circle them.

11. Ask the class for combinations (if appropriate) of the best solutions to be used toward the final solution.

12. Have the class decide on a final solution. Say, "With whom can we share this so that it can make the most impact?" List every suggestion.

13. Have the class create a plan of action which may involve writing to the president of the country in the article, writing to the UN, writing to the newspapers, etc.

14. Follow through with a plan of action.

15. Follow-up: Display any articles or letters you receive back and send copies to your principal, superintendent, and the parents of your children.

LETTER TO PARENTS
Learning the Skills of Peacemaking
Lesson 48

Dear Parents,

As part of *Learning the Skills of Peacemaking*, we will be doing a current events lesson on a global problem. Could you assist your child in finding a current events article focusing on a global issue that your child can understand? Please avoid any article that's controversial or that depicts excessive violence. Could you go over the article with your child (read it to him/her if necessary), and make sure your child knows the names of the countries involved and the nature of the problem? In class the children will be "brainstorming" solutions to global problems.

Thanks, as always, for your help.

Sincerely,

_____
Teacher

_____
Date

"I MESSAGES/YOU MESSAGES" IN GLOBAL ISSUES

OBJECTIVES

- The students will act out being people from the country they discussed in Lesson 41.

- The students will use "I/You Messages" in communicating with one another.

- The students will determine which mode of communication works better in dealing with global issues.

MATERIALS

- Win/Win Guidelines poster from Lesson 10

- Peacemaking Logs

- The article discussed in Lesson 48

PROCEDURE

1.   Have the children form a circle. Refer to the article. Say, "What was the problem we discussed in our last lesson? Who were the leaders or people involved?" Discuss.

2.   Say, "Today we're going to act out being those people and we're going to use the Win/Win Guidelines to try to work out the problem. We will pretend that we are the actual people involved."

3.   Choose several children to come to the center of the circle.

4.   Say, "There's one change I'm going to make in the Win/Win Guidelines before we begin. Instead of using 'I Messages,' I want you to use 'You Messages.' Who remembers the difference between 'I' and 'You' Messages?" Discuss. "Who can give an example of each?" Have several examples given.

5.   Review the Win/Win Guidelines and proceed with the enactment of the global conflict.

6.   After the enactment, talk about the interaction. Ask the class and the players how using "You Messages" affected the outcome. Discuss.

7.   Do the enactment over again using the same children or different ones. This time have them use "I Messages."

8.   Talk about how the use of "I Messages" changed the outcome of the conflict. Have the class compare the effectiveness of this enactment with the first one.

9.   Encourage the class to draw conclusions as to which mode of communication, "I" or "You" Messages, would work better in global level communication.

10. Have the class write in their logs about the process they just did, and the understandings that came out of it.

WE ARE ALL DIFFERENT FROM DIFFERENT PLACES

OBJECTIVES

- Each child will begin to determine his own ethnic background.

- The children will work with relatives or parents in finding out about their "roots."

- The children will begin research projects on at least one country from which their ancestors originated.

- The children will begin to understand that their families represent many different backgrounds.

    NOTE: This lesson, along with Lessons 43 and 44, correlates with Bulletin Board 10 entitled, "Roots Feed the Tree of Life." Hang the tree and the words prior to beginning this lesson.

MATERIALS

- Note to Parents (see page 196)
- Research project contract (see page 195)
- Map or globe

PROCEDURE

1.   Hand out notes to parents and the research project contracts.

2.   Go over the contracts and notes, filling in blanks together. Clearly post the project due date in the room.

3.   Refer to the Tree of Life bulletin board. Say, "America is unique in that all of its people originally came from or 'originated' in other places." Explain the word "originated." Tell the children that during the next lesson they will each get a notecard where they will write the name of the country/countries from which they originate. Let them know that their parents will help them with this tonight. Tell them the notecards will be hung on the "Tree of Life" bulletin board during the next lesson.

4.   Explain that most people in the United States are the combination of many different backgrounds. Tell the students about your own ethnic background and the countries from which your ancestors originated. Locate these countries on the map.

5.   Ask the students if any of them know about their ethnic origins. Go over the meaning of the word "ethnic." Have those children who know their ethnic background locate the countries from which they originated on the map or globe. Stress, "We are all a part of the human family. We are all interconnected, even to people we don't know. We may have cousins and relatives who still live in other countries. Maybe someday we will meet them. Maybe some of you already have." Discuss.

6.   Remind the children that they will find out about their roots from their parents or other relatives. Tell them they need to return the Parent Note with the information about their background in two days. Tell them that when they present their reports to the class they can bring in anything they have to illustrate their backgrounds: pictures, books, articles of clothing, coins, dolls, pictures of relatives who immigrated here. Tell them that as an optional activity they can bring in a native food (enough for the class to taste) on the day of their presentation.

7. Tell the children they will be locating more "countries of origin" on the map in the next lesson. Make sure the children fully understand the term "countries of origin."

NOTE: Children of mixed ethnic backgrounds should choose one country to research. Any child unsure of his/her background can either research the appropriate continent or research our state.

RESEARCH PROJECT CONTRACT
Learning the Skills of Peacemaking
Lesson 50

I, _____ , agree to complete my research

project on: _____ by _____.

date

I agree to get the help I need to complete this assignment. I also agree to speak to my teacher if I have any problems.

Signature _____

Date _____

NOTE TO PARENTS
Learning the Skills of Peacemaking
Lesson 50

Dear Parents,

As part of *Learning the Skills of Peacemaking,* your child will be completing a written project on one country from which his/her ancestors originated. Please help your child list the name(s) of the countries in his/her ethnic background on the attached form and return it by _____. If your child's background includes several different countries, only one will be chosen to work on. If you are uncertain of your ancestral roots, your child can do research on our state or the continent your ancestors came from. In order to complete the project, your child will need the following information:

- A map of his/her country of origin to copy from a book, encyclopedia, or from an actual map

- On what continent is the country?

- What does the flag look like? Have your child draw it.

- What kind of native dress does the country have? Describe it. Draw or make an example.

- What are the native foods? As an optional activity you can help your child prepare an ethnic dish to bring to school on the day of his/her report presentation.

- What other interesting facts can your child tell us about his or her country of origin?

- Could you please help your child gather the necessary information? The report should be written in his/her own words. Suggested length is ____ pages.

Thank you,

_____
Teacher

COUNTRIES OF ORIGIN
Learning the Skills of Peacemaking
Lesson 50

Child's Name _____

Country(ies) of Origin _____

_____

_____

_____

_____

_____

_____

_____

I will help my child locate information about his/her country of origin. I understand that his/her completed project is due on:_____

I will send in an ethnic dish:

Yes _____ No _____

_____
Parent's Signature

Please return this note to school.

Bulletin Board 10
Learning the Skills of Peacemaking

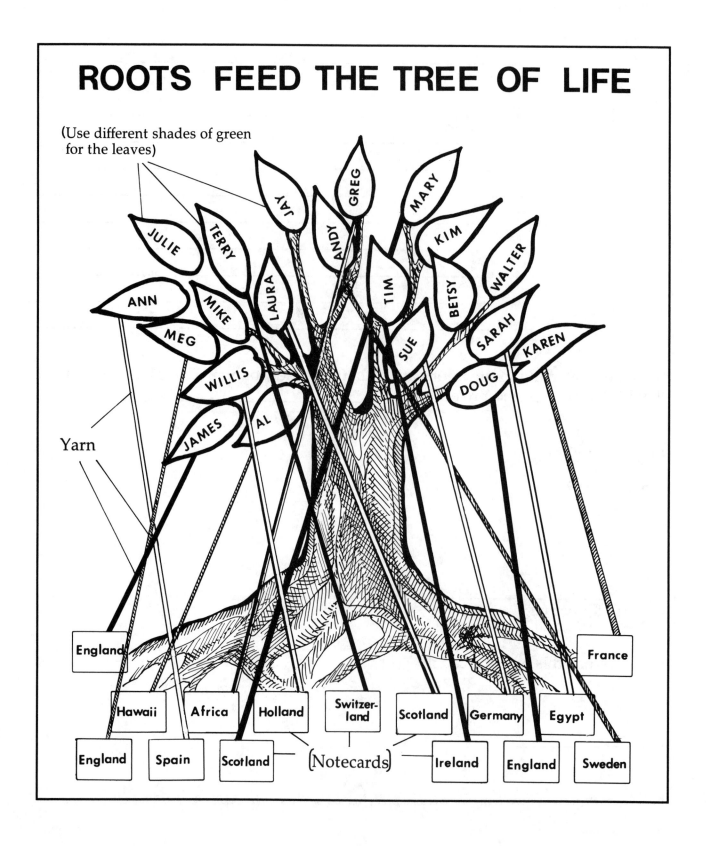

Countries Of Origin

OBJECTIVES

- The children will locate countries of origin on a map or globe.
- The children will understand that there are people with many different backgrounds in their own classroom (neighborhood, country, world).

MATERIALS

- "Countries of Origin" papers from Lesson 50
- A notecard for each child
- World map or large globe
- Yarn, clay, labels
- Large paper entitled "We Are From Many Different Places"
- "Tree of Life" bulletin board

PROCEDURE

1. Have the children sit in a circle. Say, "We all have relatives or ancestors who came to the United States from other lands." Remind them that these lands are called "countries of origin." Say, "You brought notes home a few days ago asking your parents to help you determine your countries of origin." Go around the circle and have the children name their countries of origin. Have each go to the map and locate one of his/her countries of origin. Hand each child a notecard after he/she does this, and instruct him/her to write the name of that country on the top left. This will be the country he/she will research. Underline it. Beneath it have the child write his/her other countries of origin. Have the children write their names on the top right. In Lesson 50, these notecards will be hung on the "Tree of Life" bulletin board. Refer to the bulletin board and show the children where their cards will be displayed.

2. Have each child attach a piece of yarn (with clay on each end) to the United States and the country of origin he/she will be researching. By the end of the lesson, there should be a piece of yarn for every child's selected country of origin.

3. Complete the poster "We Are All from Many Different Places" by listing the children's names and all of their countries of origin. Explain that even though each child will only be researching one country, all of his/her countries of origin will be recorded on the chart.

4. Say, "We are all part of one earth. We are the human family. Our ancestors came to the United States from other countries. We now live in harmony in America, just as people of the whole earth may someday live in harmony." Ask, "What does living in harmony mean to you?"

LIVING IN HARMONY

OBJECTIVES

- The children will explore the concept of living in harmony.
- The children will explore the concept of the UN as an instrument of harmony.
- The children will further explore their roots and interconnectedness.

MATERIALS

- "We Are All from Different Places" chart
- Encyclopedia: "United Nations" section
- "Tree of Life" bulletin board, including a leaf with the name of each child, and yarn
- Notecards the children have filled out with name of country they are researching and their other countries of origin
- Globe with clay and yarn attached
- Chalkboard, chalk

PROCEDURE

1. Have the children sit in a circle. Go over the "We Are from Many Different Places" chart, stressing the broad background of the class and how many countries they represent.

2. Draw the analogy to musical harmony, in which different instruments work together to make one unified sound, yet each participating instrument is inherently different. Make sure the children understand this analogy.

3. Briefly discuss the UN as "an instrument of harmony." Using the encyclopedia, show children pictures of the UN. Describe its function.

4. Say, "We work together in harmony in our class. Many of us are from different backgrounds, but in many ways we are alike." Ask, "How are we alike?" Discuss. List common qualities on the board.

5. Refer to the notecards mentioned in Lessons 50 and 51 on which the children have written their countries of origin. Have each child come to the "Tree of Life" bulletin board and hang up their notecards.

6. Continue to talk about the class members' diverse backgrounds. Draw parallels among members of the class, noting children's similar roots. Also note the diversity and how rich the class is in different cultures. Remind the children of the due dates of their completed projects. Tell them that they will be presenting their reports orally to the class. Remind them to bring in any objects, pictures, or artifacts that relate to their countries. Remind them also to bring in their ethnic foods at this time if they have chosen to do this optional part of the report.

> NOTE: Have a special area set aside in the room for the children to display their projects and matching artifacts, etc. Indicate to the children that everything they bring in will be displayed.

7. Have the students look at the "Tree of Life" bulletin board, now complete. Say, "Notice all of the different countries we come from. The Tree of Life is like our country and our earth. We are all interconnected."

ORAL REPORTS: OUR COUNTRIES OF ORIGIN

OBJECTIVES

- The children will deliver their oral reports on their country of origin.

- The children will gain a deeper understanding of the diversity of their backgrounds.

  NOTE: This lesson can take several days, allowing a group of children each day to present their reports. This is recommended if the reports tend to be lengthy so the class doesn't get bored.

MATERIALS

- Children's reports and related visuals

- Map/globe

- Optional—paper plates, napkins, plastic forks, or spoons

PROCEDURE

1. The children can either remain in their seats or form a circle for the delivery of the oral reports. Tell them that every child will get a turn to present their report, and that the rest of the class is invited to ask questions or provide added information during each presentation.

2. Have each child deliver his/her report. Have him/her locate the country he/she researched on the map or globe during the presentation.

3. If the children have brought in ethnic foods, have them serve the food after the report has been presented.

THE LADDER OF PEACEMAKING

OBJECTIVES

- The children will understand the hierarchy of peacemaking.
- The children will understand the connection between individual and global acts.
- The children will be guided to take responsibility for the world beyond themselves.

    NOTE: This lesson correlates with Bulletin Board 11 entitled "The Ladder of Peacemaking."

MATERIALS

- Chart:

> "Things You Can Do To Express Peacemaking":
>
> - Treat others as you want to be treated.
> - Accept others.
> - Work together cooperatively.
>   Solve your conflicts non-violently.
> - Be aware that we are all part of the same human family.

- Copy of The Bill of Rights from the encyclopedia
- Eight pieces of paper in graduated sizes, with the following written on each from smallest to largest:

    The Individual

    You & Me

    Us (small groups)

    Our Community

    Our Country

    Our State

    Our Continent

    Our World

- Masking tape to be used to attach the nine papers

PROCEDURE

1. Have the students sit in a circle. Direct the students' attention to "The Ladder of Peacemaking" bulletin board.

2. Say, "The ladder represents peace in the world and how we play a part in getting there.

Think of yourself as the person holding up this ladder." Ask, "What would happen if you let go of the ladder?" (It would fall down.) Say, "So it is with peacemaking. Individuals need to take responsibility for having a peaceful world. The individual is the foundation of a peaceful world. At the base of the ladder you can enable peace to happen at many different levels:

- within yourself
- with others
- in your communities
- in your state, country, and in the world

3. Point to the next level of the ladder, "You and Me." Show the chart: "Things You Can Do To Express Peacemaking." Discuss these concepts.

4. Say, "Let's look at the next step on the ladder, 'Us.' This step stands for the fact that you as an individual can make a difference in small groups." Ask, "What are some of the small groups you are involved in?" Refer back to the chart, "Things You Can Do To Express Peacemaking." Have the children relate the concepts on the chart to the way they interact in small groups. Talk about cooperation and acceptance at this level.

5. Focus on the next step of the ladder, "county, community, state, and country." Guide your students to see that they have a contribution to make at each of these levels, and they have already done this through some of the activities in other lessons. Discuss. Ask, "How can you take responsibility and get involved in the workings of your community, state, and country?" This is a good place to stress letter writing, knowledge of current events, attending town meetings, voting.

6. Ask about "the right to vote." Ask what this means. Discuss the privilege the citizens of this country have to cast their vote, and to have a say in the course of human events.

7. Refer to this country's Bill of Rights. Show a picture of it from an encyclopedia. Briefly explain what it means. Paraphrase each "right" to your class. Discuss. Say, "Being a peacemaker means exercising one's rights. Through this we are both taking responsibility for and making a contribution to the world around us."

8. Move up to the top of the ladder—"Our Continent and Our World." Define the term "global citizen" as someone who is part of the whole human family. Say, "Being a global citizen means that we are all citizens of the planet earth. We are interconnected, we share the earth together. Through our ability to communicate with one another we can actually be in touch with people across the globe." Ask, "What are some of the forms of communication we have that connect us globally?" (Some responses might be: TV, radio, computers, satellite communications, the mail, air travel, the telephone.)

9. Say, "It's possible to share information and even to solve problems together through joint efforts. What are some of the global problems we could work on together?" (Some responses might be: hunger, war, poverty, homelessness, diseases, pollution, crime, illiteracy.) Ask, "How can you make a difference in any of these areas?" Discuss.

> NOTE: This is a great time to pick a class project which will enable the children to address global problem-solving. Choose the problem of greatest concern to the class. Brainstorm "action steps." Decide when to begin the project.

10. Pass the nine pieces of graduated sized paper to different children. This is done to reinforce the concepts you just went over on the bulletin board. Have each child read the caption on the paper. Ask the children to arrange the papers on the floor in the order indicated through the "Ladder of Peacemaking" discussion.

11. When the papers are arranged in the correct order, hand strips of tape to other students and have them transfer the papers to the wall. Hang the papers up in order. A "free time" activity can be having two children at a time point to each paper, discussing how they personally can express peacemaking at each level.

12. In concluding the lesson, guide the class to reiterate that each segment of the hierarchy or "Ladder of Peacemaking" depends on the one preceding it, and the individual is at the foundation.

Bulletin Board 11
Learning the Skills of Peacemaking

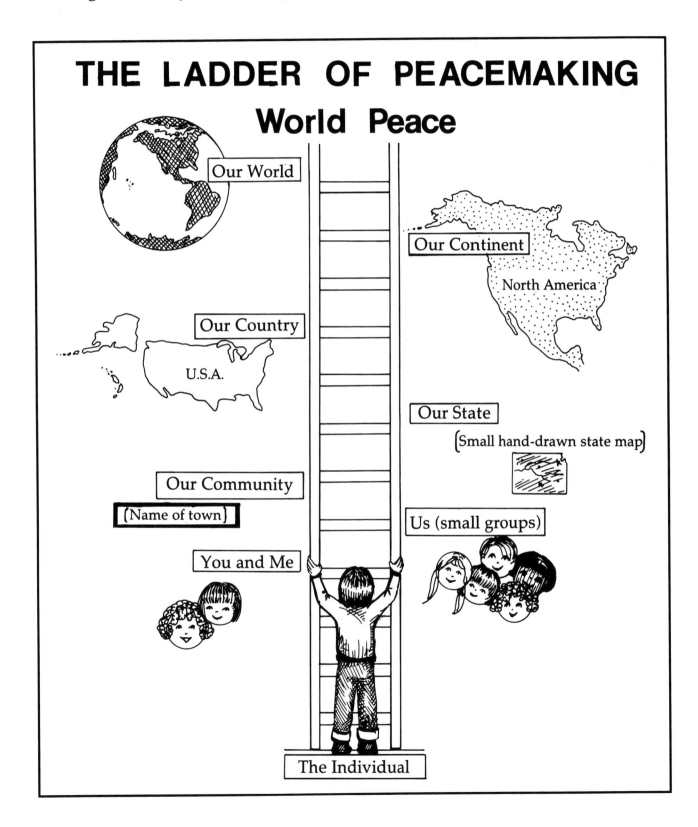

THE LADDER OF PEACEMAKING
World Peace

Our World

Our Continent

North America

Our Country

U.S.A.

Our State

(Small hand-drawn state map)

Our Community

(Name of town)

Us (small groups)

You and Me

The Individual

WE ARE DIFFERENT, WE ARE THE SAME

OBJECTIVES

- The children will identify differences and similarities in each other's thinking during a conflict resolution exercise.
- The children will use the technique of play acting in problem-solving.

MATERIALS

- Clipboard, paper, pens

PROCEDURE

NOTE: Do steps 1 and 2 first thing in the morning. The rest of the lesson is done at the end of the day.

1. Say, "As global citizens we must always be aware of our individual responsibility in solving conflicts that come up between us. Today we're going to learn a new way of doing this."

2. Say, "When you have difficulty solving a problem with another member of the class you may sign up on this clipboard [hold up]. Please write the date, your name, the name of the other student involved, and a brief statement of your problem, without placing blame."

3. At the end of the day have the class gather in a circle. Bring the clipboard into the circle.

4. Say, "How many of you have had a conflict today and signed up on the clipboard? What did you do to solve your conflict?" Give time for discussion. Talk about what worked, what didn't work. Say, "We're going to use a new technique for problem-solving and conflict resolution. This time you can pretend to be the other person so that you can see the problem from someone else's point of view." Refer to the clipboard.

5. Say, "Today _____ and _____ had a conflict. Please come to the center of the circle. Now _____ pretend to be _____ and _____ pretend to be _____ . You are going to switch places and act out the conflict."

6. Guide them in acting out what they perceived the other person to be doing and feeling.

7. When this is complete let both students sit back down in the circle. Have the class discuss what happened. Talk about how people may have different points of view but we all want to be loved and respected by others.

8. Guide the children to recognize that although people may have differences, they can resolve problems by seeing the other's point of view. Let the children who switched places tell what they realized when they pretended to be the other person.

9. Try this technique as often as you wish. You can have the clipboard and play acting time as an ongoing part of your class activity. Some teachers do this several times a week.

BEING GLOBAL CITIZENS

OBJECTIVES

- The students will represent different foreign countries in groups.

- The students will work collaboratively to determine the most important needs on a global scale for the country they represent.

- The students will act as foreign ministers of the countries they represent.

- The students will reach an agreement, as a class, on priority global needs and their solutions.

    NOTE: Each child needs a current events article prior to this lesson. You may wish to draft a note to parents ahead of time asking them to assist their child in locating an article dealing with a foreign country, determining the problem, and perceiving the needs of the country.

MATERIALS

- Student's current events articles dealing with a foreign country

- Large chart paper and markers for each group of five

- Peacemaking Logs

- Paper and pencils for "Foreign Ministers"

- Chalkboard, chalk

PROCEDURE

1.   Have students bring their current events articles to the circle.

2.   Ask each child to briefly tell about the article, including the country it focuses on, the problem outlined, and any perceived needs that country might have.

3.   Choose four or five different countries featured in the articles. Go over the problem described in each article. Write the name of each country on the board. Beneath it, write the problem referred to in the article. Divide the class into teams representing each of the countries listed on the board. Give each team chart paper and a marker and a paper and pencil for the foreign minister. Have the team pick a leader who will record information and a "Minister of Foreign Affairs."

4.   Create the scenario: "You are getting ready for a special meeting at the United Nations dur-ing which you will be speaking to representatives of other countries about the most pressing world problems and how to solve them. You will be given an unlimited amount of money to solve whatever problems you see as the most crucial for the world in general. In your group, choose the top three world problems and a proposed solution for each of them. Try to remember what the special problems of your country might be. After eight minutes we will stop." Distribute the chart paper and markers. Have the children write the name of the country they are representing on the top of the chart. Beneath it have them write what they perceive to be the three most pressing global problems. They should be thinking in terms of the country they are representing as well as general global problems. The children should be encouraged to draw upon their knowledge of urgent world problems such as hunger, disease, violence, etc.

5.   Allow time for the groups to discuss, brainstorm, and record the problems. Then ask them to list the top three problems and a possible solution for each. Circulate and help mediate differences as they arise. Foreign minister lists everything on his/her paper.

6.   After eight minutes say, "Now we're going to listen to the list of problems and solutions each country has come up with." Have each group leader share the problems and solutions.

7.   Say, "Now each Foreign Minister will visit one other country (group) and discuss the lists drawn up, seeing if the country you visit agrees or disagrees with your list. At the end of this activity we will make an imaginary visit to the UN with the lists and decide as a group on the top three world problems and proposed solutions."

8.   Give the Foreign Minister five minutes to visit other "countries." Countries can make changes in their lists at this time.

9.   Now have the class play act being at the UN. They can sit in groups representing their country. Let foreign ministers present revised lists and explain the process they went through in revision.

10. Ask the class (UN delegates) to vote on the top three global problems and solutions for them. Have them discuss the process used to get to this point of agreement or disagreement.

11. Ask, "What must it be like for real UN delegates in working to solve global problems?"

12. Students write in their logs and describe how they felt during this process. Was it difficult to come to agreement with others in and out of their own group? What worked? What didn't work? Do they think it's possible for real countries to work out their differences?

MURALS: A WORLD AT PEACE

OBJECTIVES

- The students will imagine a world at peace.
- The students will combine their individual ideas into two unified class murals.

MATERIALS

- Two or three large mural papers—one piece for each group of twelve students
- Pastel chalk, markers, crayons, paint

PROCEDURE

1. Have the children sit in a large circle. Say, "Today we are going to think about what the world would look like if it were perfectly peaceful." Say, "Think about your neighborhood this way — peaceful in all aspects with the environment being cared for, also. Think about our country at peace, with all the people being taken care of."

2. Say, "Now, think about our earth—whole, beautiful, and peaceful. Think about the people of the earth as one big family—the human family. Think about the children of different countries playing together. Think about yourself with them. I'm going to give you a moment to think about in your mind your idea of a world at peace."

3. Ask: "What did you see?" Discuss.

4. After the children have had sufficient time to share say, "Now we will form two large groups to work together in creating a mural of your ideas of a world at peace." Ask the children to select group leaders. Say, "The creation of these murals will reflect your ability to work together as peacemakers. You will want to combine all your separate ideas into one unified whole in each mural. Work with your group leader to determine together what the basic elements of your mural will be (sun, horizon line, mountains, water). Please don't

put down anyone's ideas. See how well you can combine many different ideas, and have them all fit together."

5. Distribute mural paper and materials. Say, "Each of you will get to express your own ideas of peace in these murals. But all separate ideas should flow into one unified theme. If someone's idea is different than your own, allow it to be and consider the possibilities this idea has for working with your own."

6. Stress that the creation of these murals is a peacemaking activity. It involves different people working together, sharing ideas, and solving problems as they arise. Say, "Perhaps peace will come to the world when all people can work together cooperatively."

7. Have the groups discuss ways they will execute their murals. You can "coach," but all the creating and the problem-solving should come from the children.

8. Allow the children to take as long as they need. Set aside an afternoon for this project if needed, or have the class work on the murals for several consecutive days. Clean-up should also be a collaborative activity.

9. Follow up when the murals are completed: call in the local newspapers to take pictures and then display the murals in the school library.

DESIGNING A WORLD FLAG

OBJECTIVES

- The children will work cooperatively in groups to create and design world flags.
- The children will describe what they feel is needed to have a world at peace.

MATERIALS

- Chart entitled "This is What's Needed to Have a World at Peace." (Children's ideas will go here.)
- Four or five large white papers (suggested size: 3' x 4'), for flags
- Crayons, markers, rulers, paints
- Camera, film

PROCEDURE

1. Say, "We have learned about the different countries from which we originated and the different flags of many lands. Today we're going to make world flags. They will be your creation entirely. We're also going to make a chart describing what we feel is needed to have world peace. Pictures of our flags and copies of our chart will be mailed to the Secretary General of the United Nations. In a moment we'll be dividing into groups to do this."

2. Say, "Before we begin I'd like to know why you think we don't have a world flag already." Discuss.

3. Ask the class if they think it's possible to have all of the countries of the world getting along in their lifetimes. Discuss.

4. Say, "What do you think will help us to have a world at peace?" List the ideas on the chart "This is What's Needed to Have a World at Peace." As you are doing the chart together, guide the children to the concept of individual responsibility. Also, guide them to recall the concept of human interconnectedness.

5. After you have completed the chart, say, "Imagine a flag representing all people and all countries. What would it look like?" Have the children think for a few moments about this.

6. Now have the class divide into four groups. Give each group a piece of paper and markers, etc. to create their flag. Have the children discuss their ideas together. Give them about five to ten minutes to come up with a design concept for their flag.

7. Have the groups design their flag together. Give them about twenty minutes to do this, having the members of the group decide how to execute their ideas.

8. When each group completes their flag, take a picture of it. Have the class write a letter to the Secretary General of the United Nations telling about the program they've been participating in this year. In the letter, have the children describe how they came up with their idea for the world flag. They can also include suggestions they have for having a world at peace. When you mail copies of the letters and pictures of the flags be sure to include a copy of the chart "This is What's Needed to Have a World at Peace."

9. The address to send everything to is:

   Secretary General
   United Nations
   New York, NY 10017

   Good Luck!

COMMITMENTS FOR THE FUTURE

OBJECTIVES

- The students will make commitments stating how they will personally contribute to having a peaceful world now and in the future.

- The students will record in their logs their role in creating a peaceful future.

MATERIALS

- Chart paper entitled "What I'd Most Like to Contribute to Our World"

- Peacemaking Logs

PROCEDURE

1. Have the children sit in a circle. Say, "Our school year is ending and we have learned a lot about ourselves and our world." Ask, "What have you learned that you can do to create a peaceful future?" Discuss.

2. Ask, "Do you feel that you can make a difference in the world?" Discuss.

3. Ask, "Do you feel that you can make a contribution regardless of your age? How?" Discuss.

4. Ask, "In your personal lives, how can you create a more peaceful world?" Discuss.

5. Ask, "In your communities, how can you contribute?" Discuss.

6. Ask, "How can you contribute to your country?" Discuss.

7. Ask, "In the world, how can you contribute?" Discuss.

8. Say, "What is the largest contribution you can make to the world in which we live either as a child or as an adult? Think of the thing you most would want to accomplish to make our world a better place. Think about yourself accomplishing this."

9. Say, "Turn to the person you are sitting next to. Tell your partner what it is that you want to contribute most to the world. Describe how you would like to accomplish this."

10. Give about four to five minutes for paired sharing.

11. Have the children face each other in the circle again. Each child shares about the contribution he or she most wants to make to the world. Record each child's response on the chart "What I'd Most Like to Contribute to Our World."

12. Ask the children if they would be willing to commit to living this idea of contribution. Say, "When we take a stand to do something important, that's the beginning of making it really happen. When we write down our commitments it is even more powerful."

13. Say, "Today is our opportunity to take a stand for the future."

14. Ask your children to write their commitments to the future in their logs. Give them the opportunity to read their commitments aloud. Acknowledge each child for his/her courage, vision, and uniqueness.

15. Say, "Remember, you are the key to a peaceful world."

16. Read the following quote by Goethe:

> "Whatever you do, or dream you can do, begin it. Boldness has genius, power and magic in it."

MEASURING THE UNDERSTANDINGS LEARNED IN THIS GUIDE

STAGE III: Exploring Our Roots And Interconnectedness

NOTE: Teachers, you can do this as a recap and review, or you can put these questions on a worksheet to use as a post test.

1. Define:

   conflict resolution

   countries of origin

   United Nations

   harmony

2. Tell what the Win/Win guidelines are in your own words.

3. Do you think mediation can help settle disputes? Why or why not?

4. How are you like other people?

5. Describe the Ladder of Peacemaking.

6. What kind of contribution do you plan to make to the future of our world?

7. If you could speak to our President, what would you say?

PROGRAM EVALUATION

Pre- /Post-Survey for Students Date _____

Directions: Make a check by the answers that best apply. You can pick more than one answer for each question. Be honest. You do not have to put your name on this paper. Please fill in every section. Your answers are very important to us. (Please use the back of this sheet or another if needed.)

1. What do you usually do when another child gets you angry?
   _____ hit, punch, or push
   _____ ask for help in solving the problem
   _____ name-call
   _____ curse
   _____ tattle
   _____ cry
   _____ try to talk it out with the person
   _____ walk away and dislike the person
   _____ walk away and forget about it
   _____ talk behind the person's back
   _____ give an "I Message"
   _____ find a way to get even
   _____ try to understand the other person's point of view
   Other; explain: _____

2. Do you feel most of the kids in this school treat each other with kindness and respect?
   _____ usually
   _____ often
   _____ sometimes
   _____ rarely
   _____ never

   Explain:

3. Do you feel that most of the kids in this school respect each other's ethnic differences?

_____ usually   Comments:

_____ often

_____ sometimes

_____ rarely

_____ never

4. Has anyone in this school ever said anything bad to you about your race, color, religion, or gender?

_____ yes   Comments:

_____ no

5. Have you noticed kids in this school saying bad things about other people because of their race, color, religion, or gender?

_____ usually

_____ often

_____ sometimes

_____ rarely

_____ never

Explain:

6. Do you believe we have a peaceful school?

_____ always

_____ most of the time

_____ sometimes

_____ rarely

_____ never

Explain:

7. What would make it more peaceful? Explain:

Post-Survey Only

1. What changes have you seen in the way people treat each other in our school since we began the peacemaking program? Explain:

2. Do you feel children are fighting less?

_____ yes

_____ no

Explain:

3. What are you doing differently since we began the peacemaking program? Explain:

4. Are the teachers and other adults in our school helping you handle your conflicts any differently now? Explain:

CONCLUSION

William Ryan, writer and Associate Secretary for Public Affairs, USCC, stated:

> *The same values that commit one to be a peace-maker will be the values that impel one to foster the integral development of every human being and of all peoples.*

Each time you reach out to your children and students through words and actions, think of your reach far exceeding the walls of the home and classroom. Think of yourself impacting people all over through each interaction you have. And from this vantage point, know that each life you touch will in turn touch others, and this touching of human being to human being may well be the beginning of peace for the whole world.

BIBLIOGRAPHY

Adams, Linda, *Effectiveness Training for Women*. New York: Weyden Books, 1979.

Bickmore, Kathy, *Alternatives to Violence: A Manual for Teaching Peace to Youth and Adults*. Cleveland, Ohio: Alternatives to Violence Committee of the Cleveland Friends Meeting, 1984.

Briggs, Dorothy Corkill, *Your Child's Self-Esteem*. Garden City, New York: Doubleday, 1967.

Canfield, Jack and Wells, Harold, *100 Ways to Enhance Self-Concepts in the Classroom: Handbook for Teachers and Parents*. Englewood Cliffs, New Jersey: Prentice-Hall, Inc., 1976.

Cousins, Norman, *Human Options*. New York: W.W. Norton, 1981.

Dodson, Dr. Fitzhugh, *How to Discipline with Love*. New York: New American Library, Signet, 1978.

Dorn, Lois, *Peace in the Family: A Workbook of Ideas and Actions*, New York: Pantheon, 1983.

Drew, Naomi and Siggelakis, Gail, *Resolving Conflicts in the Elementary Classroom*. Trenton, NJ: New Jersey Department of Education, 1988.

Educators for Social Responsibility, *Perspectives*. Boston, Mass.: E.S.R., 1983.

Faber, Adele and Mazlish, Elaine, *How to Talk So Kids Will Listen and Listen So Kids Will Talk*. New York: Rawson, Wade Publishers, 1980.

Fisher, Roger and Ury, William, *Getting to Yes: Negotiating Agreement Without Giving In*. New York: Penguin Books, 1981.

Foderaro, Lisa W., "You Don't Have to Fight." New York Times, Education Life, Jan. 9, 1994.

Ginott, Haim, *Teacher and Child*. New York: Avon, 1972.

Gordon, Thomas, *Parent Effectiveness Training*. New York: Peter Weyden, 1970.

James, Muriel and Jongeward, Dorothy, *Born to Win*. Menlo Park, Calif.: Addison-Wesley, 1971.

Johnson, D.W. and Johnson, R., *Teaching Students to Be Peacemakers*. Edina, MN: Interaction Book Co., 1991.

Johnson, Roger T., "Teaching Students to be Peer Mediators." Educational Leadership, Sept. 1992.

Johnson, Spencer, *One Minute for Myself*. New York: William Morrow and Co., 1985.

Keyes, Ken, Jr., *The Hundredth Monkey*. Kentucky: Vision Books, 1986.

Knight, Michael E., et. al, *Teaching Children to Love Themselves: A Handbook for Parents and Teachers of Young Children*. Englewood Cliffs, N.J.: Prentice-Hall, 1982.

Macy, Joanna Rogers, *Despair and Personal Power in the Nuclear Age*. Philadelphia, PA: New Society Publishers, 1983.

Negotiation Journal: On the Process of Dispute Settlement. New York: Plenum Press, 1985.

Newman, Mildred and Berkowitz, Bernard, *How to Be Your Own Best Friend*. New York: Random House, 1973.

Peck, M. Scott, M.D., *The Road Less Traveled*. New York: Simon & Schuster, 1978.

Peck, M. Scott. *A World Waiting to be Born*. NY: Banton, 1994.

Pogrebin, Letty Cottin, *Stories for Free Children*. New York: McGraw-Hill, 1982.

Prutzman, Priscilla, et. al, *The Friendly Classroom for a Small Planet: A Handbook on Creative Approaches to Living and Problem-Solving for Children*. Children's Creative Response to Conflict, Box 271, Nyack, NY 10960.

Schmidt, Fran; Friedman, Alice and Marvel, Jean, *Mediation for Kids*. Miami Beach, FL: Grace Contrino Abrams Peace Education Foundation, 1992.

Thomas, Marlo, *Free to Be You and Me*. New York: McGraw-Hill, 1974.

Willis, Scott, "Helping Students Resolve Conflict." ASCD Update, Dec. 1993.

BOOKS FOR PARENTS AND TEACHERS

Axelrod, R., *The Evolution of Cooperation*. New York: Basic Books, 1984.

Azerrad, Jacob, *Anyone Can Have a Happy Child: The Simple Secret of Positive Parenting*. New York: M. Evans and Co., 1980.

Barnet, Richard, *Real Security: Restoring American Power in a Dangerous Decade*. New York: Simon & Schuster, 1981.

Bodner, Joan, *Taking Charge of Our Lives: Living Responsibly in a Troubled World*. San Francisco: American Friends Service Committee.

Brand, Stewart, et. al, *The New Games Book*. The New Games Foundation, 1976.

Buscaglia, Leo, *Living, Loving and Learning*, Thorofare, NJ: Charles B. Slack, 1982.

Carmichael, Carrie, *Non-Sexist Childraising*. Boston, MA: Beacon Press, 1977.

Comstock, Margaret, *Building Blocks for Peace*. Philadelphia, PA: Jane Addams Peace Association.

Coppersmith, Stanley, *The Antecedent of Self-Esteem*. San Francisco, CA: Freedom and Co., 1967.

Crary, Elizabeth, *Kids Can Cooperate*. Seattle: Parenting Press, 1984.

DeMille, Richard, *Put Your Mother on the Ceiling*. New York: Viking Press, 1972.

Dinkmeyer, Dan and McKay, Gary D., *Parents Handbook: Systematic Training for Effective Parenting*. Minn.: American Guidance Service, Inc./Circle Press, 1976.

Dreikurs, Rudolf, *Family Council: The Dreikurs Technique for Putting an End to War Between Parents and Children (and Between Children and Children)*. Chicago: Henry Regnery Co., 1974.

Duval, Lynn, *Respecting Our Differences*. Minn: Free Spirit Pub., 1994.

Easterday, Kate Cusick, *The Peaceable Kitchen Cookbook: Recipes for Personal and Global Well-Being*. New York: Paulist Press, 1980.

Elkind, David, *The Hurried Child: Growing Up Too Fast Too Soon*. Reading, Mass.: Addison-Wesley, 1981.

Falk, Richard, et. al, *Toward a Just World Order*. Colorado: Westview Press, 1982.

Fluegelman, Andrew, ed., *The New Games Book*. Garden City, NJ: Doubleday, 1976.

Fraiberg, Selma, *Responsive Parenting*. Minn.: AGS.

Freed, Alvyn M., *TA for Tots, Revised*. Rolling Hills Estates, CA: Jalmar Press, 1991.

Fugitt, Eva, D., *"He Hit Me Back First!" Creative Visualization Activities for Parenting and Teaching*. Rolling Hills Estates, CA: Jalmar Press, 1983.

Goodman, Mary Ellen, *Race Awareness in Young Children*. New York: Collier Books, 1964.

Gordon, Thomas, *Teacher Effectiveness Training*. New York: Peter Weyden, 1970.

Gregg, Richard B., *The Power of Nonviolence*. New York: Greenleaf Books, 1984.

Haessly, Jacqueline, *Peacemaking: Family Activities for Justice and Peace*, New York: Paulist Press, 1980.

Harrison, Marta, et. al, *For the Fun of It: Selected Cooperative Games for Children and Adults*. Philadelphia, PA: Friends Peace Committee of the Philadelphia Yearly Meeting, 1976.

Hunger Project, *Ending Hunger*, NY: Praeger, 1985.

Josephson, Harold, ed., et. al, *Biographical Dictionary of Modern Peace Leaders*. Westport, Conn.: Greenwood Press, 1985.

Judson, Stephanie, *A Manual on Nonviolence and Children*. Philadelphia, PA: Nonviolence and Children Program of the Friends Peace Committee, 1977.

Katz, Neil H. and Lauyer, John W., *Communication and Conflict Resolution Skills*. Dubuque, Iowa: Kendall/Hunt Publishing Co., 1985.

King, Martin Luther, Jr., *Why We Can't Wait*. New York: Harper and Row, 1963.

Kohl, Herbert, *Growing with Your Children*. Boston, MA: Little, Brown and Co., 1978.

Lechner, Betty, *Empowering Families: A Manual of Experiences for Family Sharing*. St. Paul, Minn.: National Marriage Encounter, 1977.

Lewis, Claudia, *A Big Bite of the World: Children's Creative Writing*. Englewood Cliffs, NJ: Prentice-Hall, Inc., 1979.

Lucas, Eileen. *Peace on the Playground, Nonviolent Ways of Problem-Solving*. NY: Franklin Watts, 1991.

McGinnis, James and Kathleen, *Educating for Peace and Justice*. St. Louis, MO: Institute for Peace and Justice, 1985.

McGinnis, James and Kathleen, *Educating for Peace and Justice: Volume 2, Global Dimensions*. St. Louis, MO: Institute for Peace and Justice, 1985.

McGinnis, James and Kathleen, *Parenting for Peace and Justice*. Maryknoll, NY: Orbis Books, 1985.

Michaelis, Bill and Dolores, *Learning through Non-Competitive Activities and Play*. 1977.

Orlick, Dr. Terry, *The Cooperative Sports and Games Book*. New York: Pantheon Books, 1978.

Paley, V., *You Can't Say You Can't Play*. Cambridge, MA: Harvard University Press, 1990.

Peace Resource Book 1986: A Comprehensive Guide to Issues, Groups, and Literature. Hagerstown, MD: Ballinger Publishing Co., 1986.

Philbin, Marianne, ed., *The Ribbon*. Asheville, NC: Lark Books, 1985.

Putnam, Lillian R. and Burke, Eileen, *Stories to Talk About: Helping Children Make Ethical Choices*. NY: Scholastic, 1994.

Rogers, Carls, *Freedom to Learn*. Columbus, Ohio: Charles E. Merrill Publishing Co., 1979.

Satir, Virginia, *Peoplemaking*. Palo Alto, Calif.: Science and Behavior Books, Inc., 1972.

Schmidt, Fran, *Creative Conflict Solving for Kids*. Miami Beach, Fla.: Grace Contrino Abrams Peace Ed. Foundation, Inc., 1982.

Shannon-Thornberry, Milo, ed., *The Alternate Celebrations Catalogue*. New York: Pilgrim, 1982.

Sharp, Gene, *The Politics of Nonviolent Action*. Boston, MA: Extending Horizon Books, 1973.

Spann, Mary Beth. *Literature-Based Multicultural Activities*. N.Y.: Scholastic, 1992.

Stanford, Barbara, *Peacemaking*. New York: Bantam Books, 1976.

Sweeney, Duane, ed., *The Peace Catalog: A Guide Book to a Positive Future*. Press for Peace, 1984.

Tolley, Howard, *Children and War: Political Socialization to International Conflict*. New York: Teachers College Press, 1973.

Wein, Barbara, J. ed., *Peace and World Order Studies*. New York: World Policy Institute, 1984.

Weinstein, Matt and Goodman, Joel, *Playfair: Everybody's Guide to Non-competitive Play*. California: Impact Publishers, 1980.

Wilt, Joy and Watson, Bill, *Relationship Builders*. Waco, TX: Word Assoc., 1978.

Woolcome, David and Gordon, David, *Peace Child: A Study Guide for Schools*. Washington, D.C.: Peace Child Foundation, P.O. Box 33168.

CHILDREN'S BOOKS

Adoff, A., *My Black Me: A Beginning Book of Black Poetry*. N.Y.: Dutton, 1974.

Alexander, Lloyd, *The King's Fountain*. New York: Harper, 1971.

Bauman, Elizabeth, *Coals of Fire*. Herald Press, 1954.

Bishop, Clarie Hutchet, *Twenty and Ten*. New York: Viking, 1952.

Bolognese, Don, *Once Upon A Mountain*. Lippincott, 1967.

Boylston, Helen, *Clara Barton, Founder of the American Red Cross*. Eau Claire: E.M. Hale, 1955.

Brandenberg, Franz; illustrated by Aliki *It's Not My Fault*. New York: Greenwillow Books, 1980.

Bunting, Eve; illustrated by Beth Peck, *How Many Days to America? A Thanksgiving Story*. Boston: Houghton Mifflin (Clarion Books), 1988.

Carlson, Nancy, *Loudmouth George and the Sixth-grade Bully*. Carolrhoda Books, 1983.

Caseley, Judith, *Harry and Willy and Carrothead*. New York: Greenwillow Books, 1991.

Chapman, C., *Herbie's Troubles*. NY: E.P. Dutton, 1981.

Charters, Janet and Forman, Michael, *The General*. New York: E.P. Dutton, 1961.

Clayton, Ed, *Martin Luther King, the Peaceful Warrior*. Englewood Cliffs: Prentice-Hall, 1968.

Coerr, Eleanor, *Sadako and the Thousand Paper Cranes*. New York: G.P. Putnam, 1977.

Cohen, Barbara; illustrated by Michael J. Deraney, *Molly's Pilgrim*. New York: Lothrop, Lee & Shepard, 1983.

Conway, Judith, *I'll Get Even*. Raintree Pub., 1977.

Cooney, Barbara, *Miss Rumphius*. New York: Viking Press, 1952.

Crary, Elizabeth; illustrated by Jean Whitney, *I'm Mad*. Seattle, Washington: Parenting Press, Inc., 1991.

Crippen, David, *Two Sides of the River*. Abingdon, 1976.

De Conde, Alexander, *Decisions for Peace*. New York: G.P. Putnam, 1970.

de Paolo, Tomie, *Oliver Button is a Sissy*. New York & London: Harcourt Brace Jovanovich, 1979.

DeCosse, Paula, *The Children's Whole Future Catalogue*. New York: Random House, 1980.

Dragonwagon, Crescent; illustrated by Dick Gackenbach, *I Hate My Brother Harry*. New York: Harper & Row, Publishers, 1983.

Durell, Ann & Sachs, Marilyn, *The Big Book for Peace*. New York: Dutton, 1990.

Duvoisin, Roger, *Snowy and Woody*. New York: Knopf, 1979.

Duvoisin, Roger, *The Happy Hunter*. New York: Lathrop, Lee and Shepard, 1962.

Eaton, Jeanette, *Gandhi: Fighter Without a Sword*, New York: William Morrow, 1950.

Epstein, Sam and Beryl, *Harriet Tubman, Guide to Freedom*. New York: Dell, 1975.

Gallomb, Julius, *Albert Schweitzer, Genius in the Jungle*. New York: Vanguard Press.

Goffstein, M.B., *Natural History*. New York: Farrar, Straus, Giroux, 1979.

Goodsell, Jane, *Eleanor Roosevelt*. New York: Crowell, 1970.

Gordon, Shirley; illustrated by Edward Frascino, *Happy Birthday, Crystal*. New York: Harper & Row, Publishers, 1981.

Greenfield, Eloise, *Rosa Parks*. New York: Crowell, 1973.

Harrison, Deloris, ed., *We Shall Live in Peace: The Teachings of Martin Luther King, Jr*. New York: Hawthorne Books, 1968.

Hamanda, Hirusuke, *The Tears of the Dragon*. New York: Parents Magazine Press, 1967.

Heine, Helme, *Friends*. New York: Macmillian (Aladdin), 1982.

Hoban, Russell, *The Little Brute Family*. New York: MacMillan, 1966.

Hopkins, Lee Bennett (compiled by); illustrated by James Watt, *Best Friends*. New York: Harper & Row, 1986.

Howard, Tracy Apple and Alexandra, *Kids Ending Hunger*. Kansas City, MO: Andrews and McMeel, 1992.

Jampolsky, Gerald, *Children as Teachers of Peace*. Celestial Arts, 1982.

Kidd, Diana; illustrated by Lucy Montgomery, *Onion Tears*. New York: Orchard Books. 1989.

Lawson, Don, *Ten Fighters for Peace*. New York: Lothrop, 1971.

Leaf, Munro, *The Story of Ferdinand*. New York: Viking Press, 1936.

Leverich, Kathleen; illustrated by Walter Lorraine, *Best Enemies Again*. New York: Greenwillow Books, 1991

Lobel, Anita, *Potatoes, Potatoes*. New York: Harper, 1967.

Luttrell, Ida; illustrated by Ute Krause, *Ottie Slockett*. New York: Dial Books for Young Readers, 1990.

Marzollo, Jean & Claudio; illustrated by Susan Meddaugh, *Ruthie's Rude Friends*. New York: Dial Books for Young Readers, 1984.

McKee, David, *Two Admirals*. Boston, MA: Houghton, 1977.

Meriweather, Louise, *Don't Ride the Bus on Monday: The Rosa Parks Story*. Englewood Cliffs, NJ: Prentice-Hall, 1973.

Meyer, Elizabeth P., *Fredrick Douglas, Boy Champion of Human Rights*. Childhood of Famous Americans Series.

Milleander, Dhorothula H., *Martin Luther King, Boy With a Dream*. Childhood of Famous Americans Series.

Moeri, Louise, *Downwind*. New York: E.P. Dutton, 1984.

Moss, T., *I Want to Be*. NY: Dial Books, 1993.

Oppenheim, Joanne, *Sequoyah, Cherokee Hero*. Mahway, NJ: Troll Associates, 1979.

Pearson, Susan; illustrated by Steven Kellog, *Molly Moves Out*. New York: The Dial Press, 1979.

Ringi, Kjell, *The Stranger*. New York: Random House, 1968.

Robinson, Nancy K.; illustrated by Ingrid Fetz, *Wendy and the Bullies*. New York: Hastings House, Publishers, 1980.

Russian Coloring Book. Students of Friend's School, 5114 N. Charles St., Baltimore, MD 21210, 1978.

Sanchez, Garcia, *La Nina Invisible*. Wensell, 1968.

Scholes, K., *Peace Begins With You*. Boston: Little Brown, 1990.

Seuss, Dr. *The Butter Battle Book*. New York: Random House, 1984.

Shedd, Charlie, *Promises to Peter: Building a Bridge from Parent to Child*. Waco, TX: Word Assoc., 1970.

Simon, Norma; illustrated by Dora Leder, *Nobody's Perfect, Not Even My Mother*. Chicago: Albert Whitman & Company, 1981.

Tree, Marie Housman, *Albert Einstein, Young Thinker*. Childhood of Famous Americans Series.

Turner, Ann; illustrated by Ronal Himler, *Nettie's Trip South*. New York: Macmillian Publishing Company, 1987.

Uchida, Y., *The Bracelet*. N.Y.: Philomel Books, 1993.

Udrey, Janice, *Let's Be Enemies*. N.Y.: Harper, 1961.

Ungerer, Tomie, *Zeralda's Ogre*. New York: Harper, 1967.

Van Leeuwen, Jean; illustrated by Ann Schweninger, *Oliver Pig at School*. New York: Dial Books for Young Readers, 1990.

Viorst, Judith; illustrated by Ray Cruz, *Alexander and the Terrible, Horrible, No Good, Very Bad Day*. New York: Atheneum, 1973.

Wagoner, Jean Brown, Jane Addams, *Little Lame Girl*. Childhood of Famous Americans Series.

Wahl, Jan. *The Animals' Peace Day*. NY: Farrar, Straus, Griroux, 1970.

Wahl, Jan, *How the Children Stopped the Wars*. New York: Farrar, Straus, Giroux, 1969.

Walker, Alice; illustrated by Catherine Deeter, *Finding the Green Stone*. San Diego, New York, London: Harcourt Brace Jovanovich, Publishers, 1991.

Waybill, Marjorie, *Chinese Eyes*. PA: Herald Press, 1974.

Williams, *Come to Russia*. New York: Warwick, 1979.

Wondriska, William, *The Tomato Patch*. New York: Holt, 1964.

Zolotow, Charlotte; illustrated by Ben Shecter, *The Hating Book*. New York: Harper & Row, Publishers, 1969.

RECORDS AND TAPES

Free to Be You and Me, Ms. Foundation, New York, NY.

"No More" Record Album Series (No More Feeling Weird, No More Feeling Cheated, etc.), Word Inc., Waco, TX 76710.

"On the Radio," by Jonathan Sprout, Sprout Records, P.O. Box 188, Morrisville, PA 19067. Songs reflect acceptance, friendship, and just plain fun.

"We All Live Together" Album Series, Youngheart Records, Los Angeles, CA.

Two Hands Hold the Earth by Sarah Pirtle (tape). Love of self, humanity, and nature are stressed in songs and stories for children. A Gentle Wind, Box 3103, Albany, NY 12203.

Under One Sky and Look to the People by Ruth Pelham (tapes). Songs reflect a vision of world peace, magnificence of the human spirit. Sumitra Productions, Inc., Box U, Charlemont, MA 01339.

We Are One Planet and *Honor the Earth* by Molly Scott (tapes). Music reflects the connection between humanity and the earth. Sumitra Productions, Inc., Box U, Charlemont, MA 01339.

We Are One with Many Voices by Carolyn McDade (tape). Songs stress our interconnectedness: "one earth, one people, one life." Surtsey Publishers, 111 Mt. Vernon Street, Newtonville, MA 02160.

RESOURCE ORGANIZATIONS

ASCD Network on Conflict Resolution, c/o Mary Ellen Schaffer, Elsie Johnson School, 1380 Nautilus Lane, Hanover Park, IL 60103; (708) 830-8770.

Children's Creative Response to Conflict Program, Fellowship of Reconciliation, Box 271, Nyack, NY 10960; (914) 358-4601.

Cooperative Learning Center, University of Minnesota, 202 Pattee Hall, 150 Pillsbury Dr., SE, Minneapolis, MN 55455-2098; (612) 624-7031.

Educators for Social Responsibility, School Conflict Resolution Programs, 23 Garden St., Cambridge, MA 02138; (617) 492-1764.

Grace Contrino Abrams Peace Education Foundation, 2627 Biscayne Blvd., Miami, FL 33137; (305) 576-5075.

National Association for Mediation in Education (NAME) 205 Hampshire House, Box 33635, Amherst, MA 01003-3635; (413) 545-2462.

APPENDIX:
BLACKLINE MASTERS AND
TRANSPARENCIES

MAKING ETHICAL CHOICES II

Sean, Patrick, and their parents are visiting Mr. and Mrs. Gold and 2-year-old Simon. Mr. and Mrs. Gold ask Sean and Patrick to take Simon into the den and play with him. They all start rough-housing and Patrick falls into an expensive lamp, breaking it. Mr. Gold comes running into the room, saying, "Is everything okay?" Patrick says, "Nobody's hurt but Simon got a little wild and ran into this lamp." He points to the broken remains. "We're sorry he did that but we couldn't stop him in time." Sean is upset, knowing Patrick is lying.

What should Sean do?

MAKING ETHICAL CHOICES II

Mr. Ruiz is giving a spelling test to the class. Karen didn't have time to study last night. The words are really hard. She doesn't want to fail the test. When Mr. Ruiz looks away, Karen realizes she can clearly see the answers on Carlita's paper. Carlita always gets A's.

What should Karen do?

MAKING ETHICAL CHOICES III

Mark and Nayeem are on the playground. It's Saturday and no one else is around. Mark says, "Look what I have, Nayeem," as he pulls out two cigarettes. "Where'd you get those?" asks Nayeem. "You know cigarettes aren't good for you."

"Don't be a baby," says Mark, laughing. "I took these out of my Mom's dresser when she went to work. She'll never know they're missing. Besides, it's cool to smoke. My mom does and so does my brother. Here, have one."

What should Nayeem do?

MAKING ETHICAL CHOICES III

Tony's invited to Josh's house after school today. Josh is one of the "cool" kids. Tony's never been invited to one of their get-togethers before. There's a big noisy group of kids all over the house. Josh's parents aren't home from work yet. When Tony goes into the kitchen, he notices several of the kids drinking liquor straight from a bottle they have gotten out of the cabinet above the refrigerator. Tony watches and asks, "What about Josh's parents?"

"It's cool, man," says Linda. "Josh's parents are gonna be late. There's no way we can get caught." She offers the bottle to Tony. He hesitates and looks a little nervous.

One of the other kids says, "Don't be a nerd, man. Have some." Tony doesn't know what to do. He knows he's only in the sixth grade and he knows drinking's wrong, but he wants the other kids to like him.

What should Tony do?

COOPERATIVE GROUP SIMULATIONS

Simulation #1

Second graders Amy and Susie are good friends. They play together on the playground every day. Today Amy decides to play with Jessica instead. When Susie asks to join in they each say "No." When the class goes inside Susie knocks Amy's books off her desk. Amy responds by doing the same to Jessica.

Amy's point of view: I like to play with Susie but Jessica's been asking me to play with her for a while now. Jessica and I had just decided to go on the seesaw together when Susie came over. There's not room for three people on the seesaw so we told Susie she couldn't play with us. We didn't mean to hurt her feelings.

Susie's point of view: Amy and I play together every day. She never told me she wanted to play with anyone else. I can't believe that she and Jessica just left me out when I asked them to play. I would never do that to Amy.

COOPERATIVE GROUP SIMULATIONS

Simulation #2

Fifth graders Jamal and Peter are very competitive with one another. Every day they each rush to be first in line. Today Jamal gets in line first. He moves out of his place for a moment to pick up a paper that fell down. Peter rushes into first place in line. When Jamal sees this, he pushes Peter out of line. Peter calls him a name.

Peter's point of view: Every day Jamal tries to be first. Sometimes he "cuts" me in line. Today he got out of his place, so I should be able to be first, right? He had no right to push me.

Jamal's point of view: Every day Peter tries to be first in line. Sometimes he "cuts" me to get there. Before, I just bent over for a second to pick up a paper, and Peter comes rushing up and gets in my spot. It's not fair for someone to do that. He had no right.

COOPERATIVE GROUP SIMULATIONS

Simulation #3

Fourth graders Luz and Stephanie never liked each other. Every time Luz walks by, Stephanie giver her a look or whispers negative things under her breath. Today Luz has had enough. When Stephanie makes a face at her, Luz grabs Stephanie's hair and pulls it hard.

Stephanie's point of view: I hate Luz. She's always been mean to me. When we were in first grade, she stole my best friend away from me, and I've never forgiven her for it. She always walks right by me and ignores me. I don't think I'm doing anything so bad.

Luz's point of view: Stephanie hates me and I don't know why. She always gives me looks and whispers behind my back. My mother told me to just ignore her, which I try to do, but she keeps on being mean to me. Today I couldn't take it anymore so I pulled her hair. I know it wasn't right, but how much can a person take?

COOPERATIVE GROUP SIMULATIONS

Simulation #4

Fifth grader Lewis has a crush on his classmate, Marcy. Marcy wants nothing to do with him. Lewis always sends Marcy notes and says things that make her feel embarrassed. Marcy usually responds by walking away. Today Lewis sneaks up behind Marcy, puts his arm around her shoulder, and calls her "Sweet thing." Marcy responds by pushing him away and saying, "Get out of here, nerd." Lewis responds by using a swear word.

Marcy's point of view: Lewis won't leave me alone. I don't want to hang out with him. I've made that clear, but he still keeps bothering me, sending me these creepy notes and sometimes even touching me. I called him a nerd just to get him off me, once and for all.

Lewis' point of view: Marcy is the prettiest girl in the class. I want to be with her. I figured she's playing hard to get and if she knows how much I like her, maybe she'd cut me a break. Before, she really shot me down in front of my friends. No girl gets away with that.

COOPERATIVE GROUP SIMULATIONS

Simulation #5

Roger's father beat him up this morning. This happens often. Roger is in a foul mood when he arrives on the school bus. In walks smiling happy Jeremy, who's always in a good mood. Roger hates Jeremy for his good moods, thinking that Jeremy's life is probably a lot better than his own. He sticks his foot out as Jeremy walks down the aisle of the bus, tripping him hard. Jeremy looks up in shock and punches Roger.

Roger's point of view: My father beats me up all the time. I can't stand living in my house. Jeremy must think he's better than me. He always has nice clothes, and his father even coaches the basketball team. I can't stand seeing that confident smile on his face every day so I tripped him. I wanted to knock him down a few pegs.

Jeremy's point of view: I'm getting on the bus this morning, not bothering anyone, and all of a sudden that kid Roger sticks his foot out and trips me. I hardly even know the kid. Why would he want to hurt me? I hit my head real hard on the edge of the seat. I was so mad I punched him.

AUTHOR INFORMATION

Naomi Drew is an author, educator, and workshop leader. She has been leading workshops in peacemaking and conflict resolution nationally since 1984 and has taught for seventeen years. Ms. Drew co-authored *Conflict Resolution in the Elementary School Classroom* and numerous articles on peacemaking.

Ms. Drew's groundbreaking work has been instrumental in bringing peace education to public schools throughout the United States. In 1988, she was awarded the prestigious Governor's Teachers Grant.

Learning the Skills of Peacemaking is being used internationally and is considered to be one of the best in its field. The book has been translated into Portuguese, Russian, Rumanian, and Hungarian and is bringing peacemaking skills to children around the world.

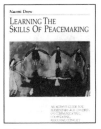

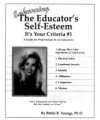

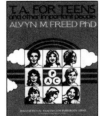

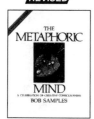